WESTRIGG
The Sociology of a Cheviot Parish

INTERNATIONAL LIBRARY OF SOCIOLOGY
AND SOCIAL RECONSTRUCTION

Founded by Karl Mannheim
Editor: W. J. H. Sprott

A catalogue of the books available in the INTERNATIONAL LIBRARY OF SOCIOLOGY AND SOCIAL RECONSTRUCTION, and new books in preparation for the Library, will be found at the end of this volume.

WESTRIGG

The Sociology
of a Cheviot Parish

by

JAMES LITTLEJOHN

LONDON

ROUTLEDGE & KEGAN PAUL

NEW YORK: THE HUMANITIES PRESS

First published 1963
by Routledge & Kegan Paul Ltd
Broadway House, 68–74 Carter Lane
London, E.C.4

Printed in Great Britain
by Staples Printers Ltd, Rochester, Kent

CONTENTS

21518

PREFACE

AND ACKNOWLEDGEMENTS

THE research on which this book is based was done mainly during University vacations between 1949 and 1951; consequently all the data refers to this period. It was written in the form of a Ph.D. thesis in 1954; this book is a compression of the thesis with much purely local detail omitted and with the addition of pages 13–25.

I thank the following institutions and persons, without whose aid the book could not have been written or published. First, the many friends I made in Westrigg; the Committee of the Social Science Research Centre, University of Edinburgh, for grants which made field-work possible; Dr K. L. Little, Head of the Department of Social Anthropology, University of Edinburgh, who supervised the original thesis; Dr W. Watson, Department of Sociology and Anthropology, University of Manchester, whose advice on the composition of the book was invaluable; Mr S. Sklaroff, Department of Public Health and Social Medicine, University of Edinburgh, for advice on statistical procedures; Dr S. F. Collins, formerly of the Department of Social Anthropology, University of Edinburgh, who drew the maps. I have also benefited greatly from the comments of Dr J. Nalson, University of Western Australia, and of my colleagues in the Social Science Research Centre and Department of Social Anthropology, University of Edinburgh. Finally, I wish to thank the Trustees of the Carnegie Trust for the Universities of Scotland for a generous subvention which has made possible the publication of this book.

J. LITTLEJOHN

Edinburgh,
February, 1963.

CHAPTER I

THE PARISH

WESTRIGG is an upland parish in a mainly rural county in the
south of Scotland. It belongs to 'the Borders', a not clearly
defined area of Scotland whose inhabitants regard themselves
as a slightly different group within the nation, different for
example in dialect and in the Common Riding ceremonies of
border towns. There are Border Associations in Edinburgh and
Glasgow for borderers exiled in these two cities. The main routes
from England north all by-pass the parish, and it is regarded as
a somewhat isolated place by people of neighbouring districts
who live nearer the main lines of communication.

It has been inhabited for several thousand years. There are
two prehistoric stone circles, several circular earth embankments
and the remains of a small Roman camp. The first general
account of the parish is given in the statistical Account of Scotland of 1791–98, which indicates that Westrigg was then
undergoing the changes in land ownership, labour organization,
and agricultural techniques general throughout the more en-
lightened parts of the country.[1] The parish seems to have contributed to the agricultural revolution. One recent author remarks
that the open drain of the hill farm which has played an
important part in the improvement of the herbage of the area
is thought to have been first used in Westrigg about 1770.[2] It is
clear from the description in the Statistical Account that by the
end of the eighteenth century the economy of the parish was
assuming the form it has retained since, the main features being
division of the land into farms devoted to sheep rearing with

[1] Sir J. Sinclair (ed.), *The Statistical Account of Scotland*, Edinburgh, 1791–99.
See also H. Hamilton, *The Industrial Revolution in Scotland*, Oxford, 1932; and
I. G. Grant, *Economic History of Scotland*, London, 1934.

[2] A. G. Ogilvie (ed.) *Essays in Regional Geography*, Cambridge, 1953.

I

individual ownership or lease of farms and hired labour paid in kind and money wages. Both in this and the later Statistical Account of 1845 the writer mentions that the local farmers are experimenting with grasses and the breeding of animals. One of these farmers is still remembered in the parish partly from a new strain of sheep he bred and partly from an encounter he had with the last witch of the parish. She turned up at his farm begging for a dish of meat. He replied that he didn't have any. She departed with the remark that he would have plenty in the morning; that night one of his cows suddenly and mysteriously died.

The only new element in the economy since then is the afforestation of about 8,000 acres of what was before sheep pasture. This began in 1939 as one of the many projects of the Forestry Commission in the borders of Scotland. The parish has undergone steady depopulation since the middle of the last century (see page 139); this has not reduced the productivity of farms, presumably because more efficient farming techniques are constantly being discovered.

The main valley in the parish is about a quarter of a mile wide and 500 feet above sea-level; from it rise hills about 2,000 feet high. It is apparent (see map 1, page 3) that the distribution of land among the farms has followed a method imposed by terrain, altitude and the necessity of growing a crop to provide winter feed for sheep. Ninety-seven per cent of the land is rough hill grazing; one of the difficulties of stock rearing in those high altitudes is relative lack of winter feed on the hills. The farms are so situated that each includes a certain acreage of fertile alluvial soil on a valley floor on which hay or some other suitable winter feed can be grown. (Few farms however are self-sufficient in this respect, and most buy hay from outside.) Each farm then consists of a few fields (mostly on the central valley floor) and large stretches of hill grazing going back to the boundaries of the parish.

Settlement is of the dispersed type (see map 2, page 4). There is no village in the parish, no shops or pubs; dwellings and the few public buildings are scattered along the valley floors with here and there a small cluster, the two most compact being forestry settlements. The two nearest towns are fifteen and seventeen miles away. Near the junction in the parish of the two roads from these towns are a post office, school and smiddy,

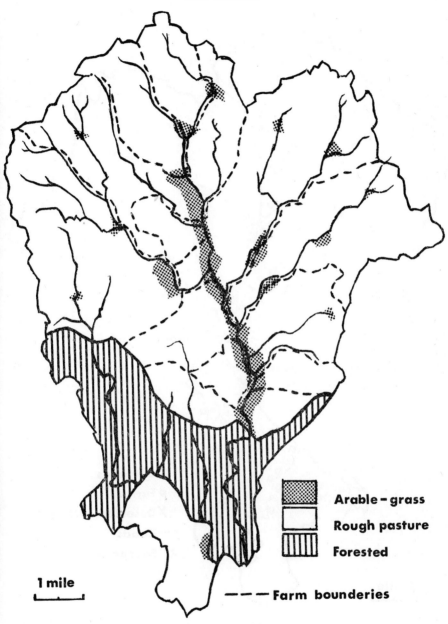

Arable - grass

Rough pasture

Forested

1 mile

— — — Farm bounderies

The Parish (1). Land utilization.

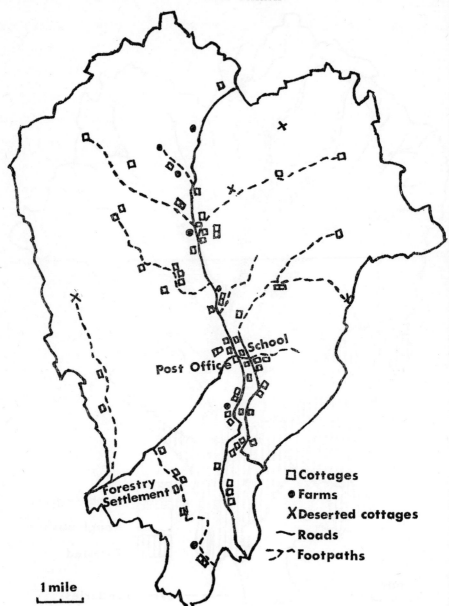

School

Post Office

Forestry
Settlement

□ Cottages
● Farms
X Deserted cottages
⌒ Roads
⌒⌒ Footpaths

1 mile

The Parish (2).   Communication and Settlement.

This, the centre of communication, is thought of by parishioners as the centre of the parish, though the geographical centre is two miles north from it. By common agreement a Public Hall was erected at the geographical centre in 1922.

The scattered settlement pattern is partly due to the requirements of large-scale sheep farming. Almost every cottage is tied, i.e., is part of the property of a farm (or the Forestry Commission now) and can be rented only if one is employed by the farmer (or Forestry Commission). The farmhouse and steading is always situated beside the arable fields and near them are one or two cottages in which live those employees whose work lies in the fields and the steading, ploughmen and general agricultural workers. A shepherd whose flock grazes on the hillsides, rising from the fields may also occupy a cottage here. The hill grazing land, however, is divided into hirstles, i.e., units each one of which is in charge of one shepherd. On the larger farms some of the hirstles lie several miles back in the hills and the shepherds in charge of them have their cottages situated on them.

However, the settlement pattern cannot be explained simply by reference to the environment and the requirements of sheep farming. The present pattern took shape under an organization of the farm in which the farm worker and his family belonged to the farm in a more strict sense than is the case now (see pages 51–55). Settlement is the feature of that organization which has remained unchanged, and there is some evidence that it is no longer adequate to the needs and desires of parishioners (see Chapter VIII).

In those farming communities in Britain already studied by anthropologists the family and kinship relationships originating in them have been found to be of the greatest importance in the local social structure, hence an account of the reasons why these do not occupy a greater place in this study seems called for. In the communities so far studied the family is so important largely because it is the unit of land ownership and of production. Rees states that 'the family farm is the basic institution of the Welsh countryside'.[1] The family farm is also at the centre of Arensberg's classic study of the Irish countryman.[2] Each family

[1] A. D. Rees, *Life in a Welsh Countryside*, Cardiff, 1951.

[2] C. Arensberg, *The Irish Countryman*, New York, 1950; and C. Arensberg and S. T. Kimball, *Family and Community in Ireland*, Cambridge, 1948.

head owns a small farm for which he and his sons supply the heavy labour while his wife and daughters look after the house and attend to the lighter work in the farmyard. Production is largely for the subsistence of the family. In both Welsh and Irish communities there is a great deal of local intermarriage while farms are inherited from father to son down the generations, resulting in a dense network of kinship ties which control the greater part of the individual's behaviour. Similarly in Gosforth in Cumberland described by Williams, 'Among farmers, and to a lesser extent in the village, the family is the unit of economic production'.[1] Seventy-three per cent of male labour on farms is provided by farmers, their families and relatives. Though Gosforth is distinguished from the other two communities in having a marked class system, Williams found that at least among farming families the rights and obligations of kinship were an important element in the social structure.[2]

Of the fourteen farms in Westrigg only one could be described as a family farm, and even on this one hired labour is sometimes employed. Farm sizes range from 454 acres to 6,600. The scale of operation on most can be judged from the fact that the American wife of one farmer calls it 'sheep ranching'. From the table of occupations it is clear that there are many more employees than farmers. These employees are all hired men and stand in no relationship to the farmer but that of employee, except in the one case mentioned of a 'family farm', where the farmer's sister, his son and himself form the labour team. Farms are often inherited but they are also sold and bought. Four farms are owned by absentee landlords and managed by shepherds.

It is clear that Westrigg is a different sort of community from those mentioned, in that kinship is a very much less important element in the social structure. As an index of the amount of kinship connections among parishioners consider first degree connections among adult householders, first degree meaning connections between ego and grandparents, parents, siblings, children and first cousins. Husband and wife are separate connecting links. Using this index, out of 96 households 57 are with-

[1] W. M. Williams, *The Sociology of an English Village*, Routledge & Kegan Paul, 1956, page 37.

[2] W. M. Williams, *The Sociology of an English Village*, Routledge & Kegan Paul, 1956, page 69.

out kinship links with others. The remaining 39 have 23
connections. Two other households are connected by affinal
bonds.

Rees remarks: 'In a community the majority of whose members were born in the same locality kinship naturally plays a
larger part than it does in modern urban communities where
kinsfolk are dispersed and a large proportion of those who work
together know nothing of one another's antecedents'.[1] This is
borne out by the fact that in Westrigg kinship ties are more
numerous among those who have lived there a long time, and
conversely the relative unimportance of kinship in the local
structure is apparent from the fact that just over half the present
population have lived there less than ten years. Table 1 below
is not completely accurate,[2] but it indicates that a dense network of kinship ties is not to be expected among this population.

TABLE I

Length of residence in parish (in years)

Age	1–5	6–10	11–15	16–20	21–30	31–40	41–50	51–60	61–70	70 +
0–15	57	15	12							
16–30	33	2	2	13	16					
31–40	31	1	2	2	3	7				
41–60	16	3	6	13	15	6	13	5		
61 +	14	3	0	5	3	6	4	4	5	4

I do not intend to imply by these figures that kinsfolk are unimportant in the life of the individual, only that the parish is not
the locus within which the kinship ties of parishioners can be
effectively studied and correlatively that a study of these ties

[1] Rees, *op. cit.*, page 73.
[2] I was not aware at the time I got this information of the extent to which
employees move from one farm to another throughout the district. The
question 'how long have you lived here?' can be answered in several ways,
e.g. by giving the total number of years spent in the place or by the number
of years which have elapsed since last moving into the place. However, despite the ambiguities in the information I think it is accurate enough for the
point I wish to make; length of residence in this table is to be understood in
the latter sense.

would not greatly illuminate the nature of the social relationships obtaining among parishioners. The two fragments of genealogies given below illustrate this point. Any adult among parishioners has more kinsfolk outside than inside the parish.

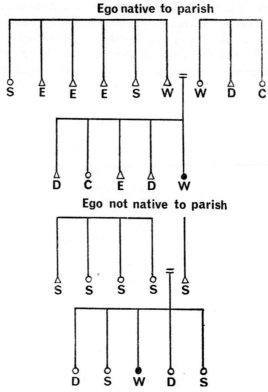

Ego native to parish

Ego not native to parish

W=Resident in Westrigg.   S=Resident in Scotland.
C=Resident in same county.   E=Resident in England.
D=Resident in a Dominion.

Outside the family the rights and obligations of kinship are neither clearly defined nor of great weight compared with those in other areas of life, particularly occupation, and no one in the parish at present owes his job to an extra-familial kinship tie. The family is the only group in the kinship system, those kinsfolk outside figuring as an assortment of relatives. This is seen in

8

the local use of kinship terminology. There is a core[1] of kinsfolk with specific denominations composed of the two families of which ego is a member in the course of his life, in which he is child and parent. Qualifiers of 'cousin' such as 'first', 'once removed', are never used and most people do not know to what categories of relatives such designations apply. Kinsfolk are most often referred to as 'freens', the term being applied both when ego does not wish to specify the precise connection he has with the referent and more often when he does not know it. The only qualifications of the term are 'far out' and 'near'. One other term sometimes used is 'kind' – 'they are the same kind'–applied to persons with the same surname associated over several generations with the same district between whom no kinship connections can be traced.

As the family is singled out in terminology so it is somewhat isolated socially, e.g., in spatial location. It is held that each family of parents and immature children should occupy a house of which they are the sole inhabitants. At marriage the spouses should leave their parental homes and parishioners are quite explicit that this is in order to free them from kinship obligations in the parental home in case these conflict with obligations and attitudes towards each other and later towards their own children. It is thought to be dangerous, or at least uncomfortable, for a young married couple with or without children to share a house with either of their parents, and especially if the parent is the householder. A few couples who had this experience spoke of the discomfort and strain of it. In one case a young husband changed his job from one with good prospects to one with none solely in order to get a house for himself and his wife though both liked the parent in whose house they had been staying.

This norm, that each family should separate itself from every other, and the fact that most cottages are tied, is responsible for a form of household composition fairly common in the district – that in which a bachelor and his retired parent or parents form the household. In most cases when a man retires from work he and his wife must live with a relative (or enter somewhere a public institution – hated and feared). A working bachelor son is the most suitable person. There are four households consisting

[1] This term is borrowed from A. Curle, 'Kinship Structure in an English Village', *Man*. Vol. LII, 1952.

of a bachelor son and both parents and two of a bachelor son and one retired parent. In all cases the retired parents have other but married children, and in all but one case the bachelor son changed his job (though not his occupation) in order to have a cottage in which his parents could live.

Rights and obligations outside the family are insignificant compared with those within. Parents are solely responsible for raising their children, are under no obligation to share their earnings with other kinsfolk and only in desperate circumstances can they call upon them for financial help. Inheritance is normally from parent to children. Whether a kinsfolk connection outside the family becomes of social significance or not is contingent upon a great many factors – geographical distance, the means to overcome it, and whether or not relatives like each other. It is understood by everyone that a connection can be 'kept up' or not, just as the parties wish, and there are several in the parish which are not. Moreover kinship connections across class boundaries are apt to be dropped.

A kinship connection outside family membership means only that the persons concerned are entitled to put forward on each other a claim to priority consideration in the way of invitations to weddings, funerals, of hospitality, and of protection against depreciatory judgment by non-relatives. Such claims are also expected to be met between friends of long standing, though there is the difference that the kinship tie confers the right to these claims while in friendship the right is only acquired as the friendship develops. In general it is women who make the effort to maintain kinship ties rather than men, women who remember exact degrees of relationship and make a point of visiting relatives.

The majority of parishioners live in Westrigg because they have sought employment there with a farmer or on the forest. They do not live there because they expect to inherit a farm in the place, as seems to be the case with a large number of the population in the communities of Ireland, Wales and England already mentioned. Every year a few people leave and others come to replace them; in 1951 six left and were replaced, in 1952 seven. The reason for moving out was either to get a more congenial job or in order to live in a less isolated district. In short, most parishioners live in Westrigg not because the parish forms a group they have to belong to or in which they have special rights, but because their occupation or that of their husband or father lies there.

So far I have been describing some of the characteristics of the population of Westrigg only in comparison to some communities in other regions of the British Isles; I turn now to a description of this population within the context of its region. The sources of the figures used below are described below; here it is only necessary to remark that they are taken either from the R.G.'s Census of 1951 or from a Census of Westrigg parish which I took in 1949. They are indicated below as R.G.'s census or own census.[1]

According to my own census the population in 1949 was 326. Occupations were:

TABLE 2

Shepherd, Shepherd Manager and Assistant Shepherd	33
Forestry employee	31
Agricultural worker	23
Millworker (females, working outside the parish)	11
Farmer	9
Housekeeper	6
Scientific Officer and Assistants	6
Postman and Assistants	4
Roadman	2
Joiner	
House maid	1
Electrican	1
Handyman	1
Minister	1
Tailor	1
Schoolteacher	1
Caretaker	1
Nursing attendant	1
Bank Clerk (working outside parish)	1

[1] Sources of the figures used in this chapter are a census of the parish I took in the summer of 1949 with the help of the parish registrar; the Registrar General for Scotland, Census of 1951; and the Census of 1951 of the Registrar General for England and Wales.

In the tables in this chapter figures for populations other than that of the parish are all from the two R.G.'s Censuses. As regards the parish there is a

By place of birth the population is fairly representative of that of the county of which it is part, as shown on Table 3.

There are two points at which there seems to be a discrepancy between the two; Westrigg has more people born in 'other border counties' and less in 'other lowland counties' than the county as a whole. There is no real discrepancy here – Westrigg is immediately adjacent to the other border counties where, like it, the economy is dominated by hill sheep farming; the county as a whole however has large areas devoted to dairy and crop farms and is adjacent to 'other lowland counties' with a similar mixed economy. In other words, both sorts of immigrants are 'local' but come from different directions. If the first three groupings – native born, other border countries, other lowland countries – are regarded as 'local' it can be said that both for Westrigg and the county the vast majority of people are locals, forming respectively 83.3 per cent and 81.7 per cent of the two populations. The case of Irish immigrants seems to show a slight discrepancy; however one would need to know the occupations of these immigrants before deciding on the matter. Irish labourers turn up in Westrigg from time to time, usually in teams of about four, to dig ditches on contract to farmers. If the Irish-born immigrants enumerated among the county population are mainly contract labourers who happened to be there at the time of the census then there is no particular discrepancy here.

One other feature of the county population must be mentioned, that is the 802 persons enumerated as born in Europe. The majority of these (I reckon) are European displaced persons,

considerable difference in the figures for total population between my census and the R.G.'s 326 and 360 respectively. The discrepancy is due partly to my having inadvertently missed two households in my census and partly to an increase in the number of forestry employees (with wives and children) in the parish between 1949 and 1951, and possibly to a few more births.

Recently the punch cards on which the R.G. (Scotland) codified the data from the 1951 census have become available to Edinburgh University for research purposes. I managed to recover 340 of the 360 for Westrigg and was glad to note that there was no discrepancy between the age – sex structure disclosed by these cards and that from my own census. As there was no discrepancy I have preferred to use my own data in Chapter I., except on Table 3 and Table 5. I used the R.G.'s census data for the parish in Table 3 because I did not have the requisite information in my own census, and in Table 5 because the data for other parishes used there is taken from the R.G.'s census.

TABLE 3

Place of Birth of Parish and County Populations

| Place of birth | Westrigg (Sample from R.G.'s Census) | | County (R.G.'s Census) | | |
	No.	Per Cent of total	Place of birth	No.	Per cent of total
Westrigg & County	182	58.3	County	53,175	62.1
Other Border counties	38	12.2		1,298	1.5
Other Lowland counties	40	12.8		14,210	16.6
Highland counties	9	2.9		1,893	2.2
Glasgow 3			2,693		
Edinburgh 7			1,315		
Aberdeen 3	13	4.2	187	4,389	5.1
Dundee 0			194		
England	28	9		7,577	8.8
Wales	2	0.6		237	.3
Ireland	0	0		941	1.1
Europe	0	0		802	.9
Isle of man and Channel Islands	0	0		25	
Commonwealth and Colonies	0	0		466	.5
Foreign Countries, British subjects	0	0		288	.3
Not stated				359	.4
totals	312	100		85,660	99.8

ex-soldiers and perhaps some ex-prisoners of war. I judge them
to be composed as follows:[1]

Place of birth	Male	Female
Russia	191	5
Poland	178	7
Germany	169	35
totals	538	47

[1] R.G. (Scotland), Census 1951.

I mention these specifically because the following pages are occupied with an analysis of urban-rural sex ratios, and it is possible that the presence of this population in the county has influenced to a slight extent the figure relating to single males in rural areas. The majority of these displaced persons are engaged in agriculture and forestry. To what extent they have married women in the county I do not know. There are no such marriages in the parish. It is certain however that there has been some intermarriage. One writer in the Third Statistical Account of Scotland remarks on it in the parish he is concerned with. Assuming that of the 500 males to be accounted for, 100 were resident in towns, and of the remainder half have married local girls, there are left 200 unmarried. I do not think this number is sufficiently large to introduce an artificial bias into the relative proportions of males in urban and rural areas.

The composition of Westrigg population by sex is unusual compared with that of the county as a whole and that of Scotland, unusual in that there is an excess of males. In 1951 (R.G.'s Census) there were 109.4 females for 100 males in Scotland, and in the county of which Westrigg is part 107.6 females for 100 males. According to the R.G.'s census, males in Westrigg exceed females by 28, and according to my own census by 31. The sociological implications of this demographic situation are somewhat important and are discussed in Chapter VIII, hence a further examination of this aspect of the population's structure seems appropriate here. Age and sex composition of all but four households in the parish (own census) is:

TABLE 4

Sex-Age Structure of Westrigg Parish

	Male	Female
0–14	44	36
15–24	26	20
25–44	44	39
45–64	41	35
65–+	20	14
totals	175	144
total sample 319		

14

This apparently anomalous composition appears less unusual when put in the context of differences between rural and urban populations of the county.[1] There is one large town (population over 20,000) and several small ones (population between 2,000 and 5,000). The normal excess of females over males is largely concentrated in the towns. In the large town the ratio is 116.1 females per 100 males, in the small towns 115.6 per 100 males and in the landward areas only 100.3 females per 100 males. Moreover, of the eight districts of the county (a district is a unit of two to five rural parishes) three show an excess of males, females exceeding in the remaining five. Westrigg belongs to one of the three districts with an excess of males.

Excess or deficiency of males seems to be associated to a large degree with differences in population density and mode of exploitation of the land. In Table 5 the rural parishes of the county are arranged according to degree of density of population, and excess of males or females in the population noted against each.

While there is no absolute rule, it is clear that the lower the density of population the more likely it is that males will predominate. Parishes No's 10, 12, 13 and 20 which seem exceptions to the general rule each includes a substantial village within its boundaries, and this perhaps accounts for the excess of women in them. The comparison of urban with rural populations shows that with higher population density females predominate. The higher proportion of males in the rural population is not due simply to an excess of males under 15, as later tables show.

The lower the population density of a parish, the more the land consists of hill sheep or upland stock farms with, in some cases, forestry settlements: the higher the population density the more it consists of dairy and crop farms. Along with the difference in mode of exploitation of land and of resultant population densities is found normally a difference in facility of access to towns for those dependent on public transport. Bus services are normally less frequent in the hill districts, but even

---

[1] This phenomenon is not confined to the county population considered here. See e.g. David C. Marsh, *The Changing Social Structure of England and Wales*, Routledge & Kegan Paul, 1958, page 21: '.... since the 1920s in both England and Wales the proportion of females to males has usually been higher in urban than rural areas and the larger the town the greater is the excess of females.'

where they are not, they cannot be uniformly available to the whole of a scattered population.

Since in the following pages Westrigg district is used as an example of an isolated district with Westrigg parish the most

TABLE 5

Parish Serial No.	Population per 100 acres	Net balance of Males	Females	Total Population
1 (Westrigg)	1	28		360
2	1	3		193
3	1	6		322
4	2	11		497
5	2	4		244
6	2	34		296
7	3	18		288
8	4	31		1,177
9	4	69		767
10	4		55	1,219
11	4	19		639
12	4		26	878
13	4		64	782
14	4	18		258
15	5	49		627
16	5	11		401
17	6	15		731
18	6	1		1,455
19	6	5		613
20	7		75	1,045
21	7	17		423
22	8	11		579
23	8		46	1,054
24	8		14	1,444
25	8		15	683
26	9		13	867
27	9	22		1,048
28	10	16		710
29	10		20	914
30	11		5	525
31	11		1	769
32	15		2	1,154
33	23		82	1,842
34	36		97	3,037
35	37		63	1,791

isolated parish in it, I had better explain the composition of the district. It consists of Parish No's 1, 2, 3 and 18; the first three of extremely low density, the latter of medium density, and a parish which does not figure in the table since it is only partly rural. This latter parish includes one of the small towns of the county. The unit 'Westrigg district' however does not include this small town, but only the landward part of the parish. This landward area is of medium population density (6 per 100 acres) and has a preponderance of 16 males in a total population of 346.

The gradient in male/female ratios from the large town through the small towns, the landward area as a whole, Westrigg district and Westrigg parish, illustrates the association of excess in number of males with low density of population. The gradient is shown for various age groups in Table 6 below: the county as a whole serves as the standard population.

TABLE 6

Urban-Rural Sex Ratios

Age	County as a whole	Large Town	Small Town	Landward Area	Westrigg District	Westrigg Parish
0–14	1.07	1.03	1.14	1.07	0.99	1.22
	1.00*	0.96	1.07	1.00	0.93	1.14
15–39	0.96	0.90	0.89	1.04	1,13	1.36
	1.00	0.94	0.93	1.08	1.18	1.42
40–49	0.95	0.88	0.82	1.05	1.27	1.20
	1.00	0.93	0.86	1.11	1.34	1.26
50–64	0.80	0.72	0.73	0.88	0.78	1.00
	1.00	0.90	0.91	1.10	0.97	1.25
65–68	0.73	0.60	0.66	0.86	1.04	1.43
	1.00	0.82	0.90	1.18	1.42	1.96

* In order to show the gradients more clearly the ratio for each unit from large town – Westrigg parish has been expressed, in the lower line in each age group, as a percentage of the ratio in the standard population, i.e., county as a whole.

My purpose so far has merely been to exhibit Westrigg parish within its proper context, showing that it represents a perhaps extreme case in some process normal to communities of its type. It is a somewhat extreme case of an upland parish with a dispersed population of low density isolated from everyday contact with towns. It was in fact because of its isolation that it was chosen for study. How parishioners assess their own situation is described in Chapter VIII. Meanwhile, having shown this, I want now to discuss these population figures in more detail.

It is perhaps best to begin by disposing of exceptions. There are two places at which exceptions to the general trend appear, one at age group 50–64 and one at age group 0–14, both under Westrigg district. The first is a minor deviation from the trend, the male/female ratio in the district is still higher than that in both large town and small towns. The second is also a relatively minor deviation but somewhat puzzling. Up to 15 years males normally exceed females in number due to excess of male births. It is possible that the practice of many of the richer farmers of sending their children to boarding schools outside the district (see page 92) has disturbed the normal ratio here. My census of Westrigg parish on which the figures for it are based was done during a school vacation when all children were at home.

Two points of sociological interest emerge from these figures. The first is the abnormal excess of males in the landward area (including Westrigg district and parish) between the ages of 15–49. There are two possible explanations for this: differential death rate and selective migration. As to the first, it is well known that the death rate of males in rural areas is lower than that of males in towns, though the difference between the two rates is gradually decreasing. The difference in the age group considered here may also reflect the fact that agricultural occupations were reserved in the last war: as Table 11 below shows, there is a remarkable excess of widows in the large town. Since, however, the difference in the sex ratio between towns and landward area increases with age and is most striking in the 65–84 age group, it is unlikely that this historical fact (though by no means irrelevant to the total picture) is of much weight compared with the two processes mentioned.

As to migration, it could be a migration of females from rural areas to towns, or of males from town to rural areas. The latter possibility is most unlikely: rural occupations and the country as an habitat are somewhat despised by the majority of townsfolk (see page 140), and no more than five of the present agricultural and forestry workmen are townsmen. The first – migration of females to towns – is much more likely. There are more diverse and attractive (see page 153) occupations in town for young girls and possibly the chances of finding a husband are better.[1] Between 1949 and 1952 four unmarried girls of Westrigg took up more or less permanent residence in town (living with a relative and coming home week-ends) but only one youth. However to what extent each process, differential death rate and selective migration, contribute to the end result could only be determined by a large scale inquiry specifically devoted to the matter.

The other point of interest in the figures in Table 6 is the variations in the difference between urban and rural ratios in different age groups. From 15–49 the female excess in large and small towns increases, while between the same ages there is an increase in the male excess in the landward area as a whole. Between ages 50–64, however, females predominate in both urban and landward areas. (It is in this age group that the effects of the First World War on the sex ratios would be most marked). The age group 65–84 shows some interesting variations. In large and small towns the female excess increases slightly, while in Westrigg district and parish males once more exceed in number.

There are several possible explanations for the reversal of the normal sex ratio (normal for the landward area as a whole in this instance) in the district and parish. The low mortality rate of males in rural areas as compared with urban might vary in different rural occupations, so that those occupations most heavily represented in upland districts might have a lower death rate than occupations in low-lying districts. The occupation most heavily represented in Westrigg and similar parishes is shepherding and next to that in Westrigg is forestry. In the low-lying districts other agricultural workers, cattlemen and horse-

[1] As regards the difference between upland and lowland rural areas (see Table 5, and pages 18–20) in male/female ratios, the excess or higher proportion of males may also be partly due to differences in the types of farming characteristics of the two areas. There are very few shepherdesses, but women are often employed as dairymaids on lowland dairy farms.

men must be more heavily represented than shepherds and foresters.

There is no direct evidence of a difference in mortality rate between these two groups of occupations in Scotland. Figures published for England and Wales, however, suggest that shepherds have a lower mortality rate than foresters and other agricultural workers, and foresters a slightly lower rate than the latter.[1]

Table 7 (below) indicates the mortality rates for the different agricultural occupations. The figures are:

TABLE 7

Agricultural Occupations – Mortality Rates (England & Wales)

Occupation	Deaths registered in 5 yrs. 1949–53	Expected Deaths	Standarized Mortality Rate	1951 Census Population
Shepherds	49	73	67	3,078
Foresters and Woodmen	253	260	97	13,397
Other agricultural workers	3,795	3,730	102	195,667

The evidence here is not too conclusive in view of the small number of shepherds compared with the others. Further suggestive evidence of differences in mortality rates in different rural occupations in Scotland is perhaps to be seen in differences in their age structures. In the 'Westrigg group', shepherding and forestry, have more men in the older age group than do the other occupations. The figures (for Scotland as a whole) are as shown on page 21.[2]

Further evidence of a difference in morality rate between these two groups of occupation is perhaps to be seen in differences between them in percentage of widowers. Since females increasingly predominate the older the age group, a higher percentage of widowers in an occupation might mean a lower death rate among the men in it. (These figures for widowers

[1] Occupational Mortality, 1951 Census (England and Wales), Decennial Supplement, H.M.S.O.
[2] 1951 Census (Scotland) Decennial Supplement, H.M.S.O.

TABLE 8

Forestry and Agricultural Occupations, Age Structures (Scotland)

Age	Shepherds	Foresters	Other Agri. workers	Cattlemen	Horsemen
15	1.12	1.46	4.74	3.23	1.28
16	1.59	2.09	5.08	4.01	2.25
17	1.09	1.99	4.27	3.76	2.62
18–19	3.42	1.89	6.37	6.06	5.91
20–24	8.23	10.82	13.10	11.05	13.93
25–29	8.05	13.49	12.16	12.87	12.79
30–34	8.75	10.17	8.82	10.38	10.71
35–44	23.52	21.57	17.24	21.57	21.45
45–54	21.49	19.20	13.35	14.27	16.52
55–59	7.96	6.75	5.04	4.87	4.91
60–64	6.88	5.38	4.65	4.09	4.80
65–69	4.43	3.20	2.84	2.08	2.03
70–74	1.89	1.18	1.59	0.85	0.65
75 +	0.95	0.73	0.68	0.28	0.14
total	100	100	100	100	100

include divorced too, but the number of divorced can be taken to be too small to affect the relative percentages). The figures for Scotland on a whole are :[1]

TABLE 9

Agricultural Occupations – Conjugal Condition (Scotland)

Occupation	Percentages in each conjugal condition			
	Single	Married	Widowed & Divorced	No's in each occupation
Shepherds	35.4	60.2	3.9	5,552
Foresters	39.8	57.0	2.8	7,551
Other Agricultural workers	57.1	39.1	3.0	31,113
Cattlemen	43.7	53.4	2.4	11,157
Horsemen	45.8	50.9	2.6	7,105

[1] 1951 Census (Scotland) Decennial Supplement, H.M.S.O.

The differences in the percentages of widowed are, however, not very great. The higher percentage of widowers among shepherds may be only a reflection of the fact that there is also a higher percentage of them married. Moreover, though shepherding and forestry have more men in the older age groups than the other occupations, this does not necessarily mean that these occupations have some beneficial effect upon the mortality rate of those in them. Countrymen change occupations: men may be attracted to shepherding and forestry work as they grow older. While I do not know of any parishioner having taken up shepherding in later years, several have changed from agricultural to forestry work. Finally, the larger proportion of men over age 65 – the 'retiring' age – in shepherding could be due to a shortage of shepherds which farmers alleviate by persuading elderly shepherds to stay on working. There is in fact a certain amount of evidence for this view, and the matter is further discussed in Chapter VIII. Meanwhile, whatever the reason for the disparity in age structure in those two groups of occupations, Tables 8 and 9 indicate that the population of Westrigg is likely to include more working elderly men, and among them slightly more widowers than would be found in the population of a low-lying rural parish.

The excessive proportion of males in the rural population, and in particular their predominance in Westrigg district and parish in the 65–84 age group, might be due less to a prevalence of males than to an absence of females. That is, it might be due to a relatively high proportion of single men in rural areas, and a low proportion of single and widowed women. The difficulty in finding evidence for this supposition is that the R.G.'s breakdown of the population into these categories by age does not go down to units smaller than the county. However, by using the method of indirect standardization (see *Note*, page 26, for a full account of this method) the ratio of expected to actual numbers in these categories was found for the units relevant here. The figures for single men are given in Table 10.

It is clear from these figures that there are proportionately more single males in the landward population than in the urban. This, of course, is not unexpected in view of the preponderance of males over females between the ages of 15–49 in the landward area. More important perhaps, the trend exhibited by

TABLE 10

Urban-Rural Populations: Single Males

Unit	Expected No.	Actual No.	Ratio Actual/Expected
Large Town	3,051	2,684	88
Small Town	1,617	1,478	91
Landward Area	5,346	5,899	110
Westrigg District	338	378	112
Westrigg Parish	43	51	119

these figures is consistent with that in Table 6 showing that males increasingly predominate (or are increasingly represented in number) with increasing low density of population and increasing isolation of locale. Hence it would seem that one reason for this trend is of a social rather than purely biological nature. It could be a disinclination on the part of women to settling down in remote localities, or that men in such localities suffer from restriction in opportunities of meeting possible wives; or it may be that such places attract 'confirmed bachelors'. There is also the possibility that the higher proportion of single males in rural areas is confined largely to the 15–24 age group. This would be consistent with the hypothesis that young girls tend to leave country districts to find jobs in towns.

The figures for widows are strikingly consistent with the trend shown in Table 11.

TABLE 11

Urban-Rural Population: Widows

Unit	No. of widows Expected	Actual	Ratio Actual/Expected
Large Town	1,154	1,428	124
Small Town	866	918	106
Landward area	2,107	1,770	81
Westrigg District	138	102	73
Westrigg Parish	17	10	59

These figures, like those concerning rural-urban sex ratios in general, can be interpreted by reference to the higher death rate of urban males and to a possible migration, in this case, of widows from less to more densely populated areas. But again, without numerical data concerning the latter, it cannot be assessed to what extent each process contributes to the final result. The reasons likely to induce young girls to leave country districts for the town are likely to induce younger widows also. For both young and elderly widows, a major obstacle to living in a country district is that most of the cottages are tied. Finally, it may be reasonably presumed that many elderly infirm widows either prefer to live in towns because medical treatment is more readily available there, or have to live in towns in those institutions intended to provide for them.

It is possible that the figures on widows are to some extent influenced by differences in census returns from rural and urban areas. It is presumably easier in a town than a country parish for a single, deserted or divorced woman to call herself a widow and to be accepted as such; it is also possible that among some sections of the population the definition of 'widow' is not the same as the official one. However in the absence of data on this subject there is no point in speculating about it.

Using the method of indirect standardization, no significant differences were found with regard to single females except in the case of small towns, where the actual number was lower than the expected. No significant differences were found with respect to widowers.

To gather together the main points from the preceding analysis and discussion – it is intended to account for the abnormal sex ratio in the population of Westrigg, the abnormality being an excess of males. The normal excess of females over males is very much lower in rural areas in general than in urban. In the county of which Westrigg is part there are three out of eight districts in which males predominate. Associated with excess of males is a complex of features: an economy based more on hill sheep farming, upland stock rearing and in some cases forestry rather than dairy or arable farming; low density of population; and an habitat remote from towns, in the sense that access to town is difficult either by reason of distance or absence of transport.

Accepted that the units large town, small town, landward area, Westrigg district and Westrigg parish represent points along a scale measuring degree of population density and of remoteness from towns, then the lower the population density and remoter the habitat, the higher the proportion of males to females in the population. Associated and consistent with this trend are two others: an increase in the proportion of single males in the population and a decrease in the proportion of widows. One other separate point emerged from the figures – an upland rural parish devoted to hill sheep farming and forestry is likely to have a higher proportion of elderly men still working than a low-lying rural parish, and there is some evidence that there is likely to be a higher proportion of them widowers. I have not attempted to assess the relative weight of the causes of the population process described: differential mortality rates, selective migration and social attitudes to isolation. In a later chapter, I attempt to describe these social attitudes and how parishioners view their situation.

The characteristics of the population must be reflected in the composition of households in the parish. From a sample of 92 households (out of 97) the following types can be distinguished:

(A) Family unit, marital core, parent breadwinner   41
     The 'normal' family. Some of course have a relative or relatives of one of the spouses living with them.

(B) Family unit, marital core, child breadwinner   7
     There are two sub-types:
     (a) the marital core are elderly, retired, and the breadwinner is a bachelor son;   4
     (b) the marital core are young, without children, and support a widowed parent;   3

(C) Family unit, marital core, no children   22
     Two sub-types:
     (a) Old. The couple's children have dispersed, or they are childless and beyond the age of having children;   15
     (b) Young   7

(D) Family unit, non-marital core   11
     Three sub-types:
     (a) Widow and child, or children;   5
     (b) Widower and child, or children   5
     (c) Siblings   1

(E) Non-family unit   11

    (*a*) Bachelor, alone, or with another bachelor, or

    with a housekeeper.   7

    (*b*) Widow, alone   2

    (*c*) Divorced man   1

    (*d*) Spinster   1

                                 total   92

Since the R.G.'s analysis of household composition in the county is concerned only with the number of persons per room, etc., I do not attempt any comparison between it and the data for Westrigg.

Note. The data used for the calculations in Tables 10 and 11 are from the report on the county by the R.G. for Scotland, forming part of his report on the Fifteenth Census of Scotland (1951). The tables from which the data are taken are those on Quinquennial Age Groups and Conjugal Conditions and on Age Distribution by Single Years and Conjugal Condition. The figures for Westrigg are from my own census. The method of indirect standardization was suggested and explained to me by S. Sklaroff, Dept. of Public Health and Social Medicine, Edinburgh University.

First, for each quinquennial age group of the county population from 20 to 99 the number of married women and of widows was found, and the ratio of widowed to married calculated. Married women rather than all females was chosen because widowhood is a condition which has relevance only in the context of marriage.

Second, for each population considered (e.g. large town, small towns, landward area, Westrigg district and Westrigg parish) the number of married women in each age group was multiplied by the corresponding ratio as found above, giving for each age group the expected number of widows.

Third, the expected number of widows in each age group of a given population were added together to give the expected number of widows for that population. This was expressed as a ratio of the actual number of widows for that population as given in the R.G.'s tables. Only the results of this last operation are presented in Tables 10 and 11.

Analogous calculations and operation were performed for Table 10. The ratio used to calculate the expected numbers of single men for each population was the ratio of single to total males in the standard (i.e., county) population.

CHAPTER II

FARM AND FOREST

THERE are no tenant farmers in Westrigg. Of the fourteen farms ten are occupied by the owner, while four are 'led', i.e., the owner resides elsewhere and the farm is in the charge of a manager. Sizes are as follows:

Farm	Acreage	Farm	Acreage
A	6,600	H	1,609
B	6,024	I	1,104
C	5,368	J	1,023
D	4,710	K	1,000
E	2,176	L	710
F	1,877	M	600
G	1,815	N	454

The number of permanent employees per farm varies from eleven to one. Most of the farmers say they could employ more than they have and at periods of heavy work or in the course of improvement projects such as large-scale drain digging it is normal to hire extra casual labour. The main income is from sheep:[1] several farmers have a secondary income from fattening hill cattle and from time to time a farmer may sell a small surplus crop of some kind. Formerly the farmer's wife made an income from eggs, from which she was expected to buy the groceries for the family. Some of the wives still make a small income in this way though whether it is spent on family groceries is doubtful. The techniques and implements used are in general use throughout the country and present no distinctive features: all the farms

[1] See Appendix 1 for a detailed description of the organization of a sheep farm.

in varying degrees use tractors, trucks, modern threshing machines, etc.

Each farm is a productive unit on its own, a business from which the farmer tries to make a profit. There is little co-operation in work among them. The occasions which give rise to most are sheep clipping and threshing. Small farms seek help oftener than large ones. Help at threshing is required on farms which do not have a modern threshing machine and which hire one from the Department of Agriculture. As they are expensive to hire farmers like to get the job done in one day and invite help from anyone who can spare the time – anyone from any farm provided his own employer permits him. No payment is given but the farmer feeds everyone present. In the next chapter I describe the disappearance of the 'clipping band'. The larger farms in the parish no longer seek outside help for clipping but a few of them regularly have it offered from one or two of the small farms, because the latter do need outside help, and get it in this way. Two farms hire outside help from the Forestry. Two pairs co-operate at clipping (A with A_1 and B with B_1). It is interesting to note that this latter instance of mutual aid which has sprung up since the disappearance of the clipping band follows class lines, one pair being of lower middle class farmers, the other of upper middle.

It is clear that there is much less mutual aid than among the farmers of Ireland described by Arensberg and those of Wales described by Rees.[1] Since in these other communities farms are very much smaller and small farms in Westrigg seek help oftener than large ones, it may seem that size of farm explains the difference. This is not altogether the case, for in those other communities the farms are family farms and kinship bonds among the families are numerous. Co-operation among them is less of an economic necessity than an affirmation of kinship bonds. The Irish countryman explains his act of mutual aid 'as part of the traditional reciprocation of sentiment and duty which makes up his system of kinship'.[2] Rees shows that assistance is part of the relationship of kinsfolk and neighbours. There are no kinship ties among the farmers of Westrigg.

[1] C. Arensberg, *The Irish Countryman*, New York, 1950, page 67. A.D. Rees, *op. cit.* chapter VIII.
[2] C. Arensberg, *op. cit.*, page 67.

In addition however there is a less tangible factor accounting for the situation in Westrigg for it is held that a man, any man, should be as independent as possible from other people (as regards business and work). This was clearly expressed in many discussions I had with workmen about smallholdings. While they all thought that in general smallholdings were a 'good idea' they objected to them on the score that they were too small to be self-sufficient. As one said: 'A farm has to be big enough so that you have everything on it. It's no use if you've always to be beholden to your neighbour. It's no use if he has a horse and you haven't and you have to run to him for a loan of it. If your neighbour starts ploughing then it's time you were ploughing too.'

This spirit is not simply due to the lack of kinship ties among the farming population; it is a positive outlook reflecting the relation between farms, for farmers, and to a lesser extent their men with them, stand in a relationship of rivalry to each other. The farmers do not farm on a subsistence basis, as seems to be the case where the family farm predominates. If the farmer can get enough money from annual profits he buys a larger farm, or another one to leave in charge of a manager, or sets up his sons on farms, or sometimes he buys a town house and retires.

It seems that below a certain size (which could only be determined by specific research) farms have to be worked on a subsistence basis. Where this is the case the family farm is the basic economic unit and any community of such farms will be characterized by numerous kinship ties and by a high value placed on neighbourliness. In such a community mutual aid will be the norm. Above this size farms become business enterprises. A community of such farms is not characterized by kinship ties among farmers, who compete with each other in the market; among them mutual aid is uncommon. (I must add that though farmers in Westrigg compete with each other they are in no sense hostile to each other, and never refuse a request for assistance from a neighbour. The point is that such requests are rare.)

The farms competing with each other in selling lambs, wool and tups are of course much more numerous than the fourteen farms in Westrigg, and a study of such competition belongs to economics. More important for this analysis is that among farmers in any one locality competition takes on the aspect of rivalry for reputation.[1] Reputation as a good stocksman is valued in itself and also gives the farmer an advantage in another area of competition, viz. for good labour.

That esteem as a stocksman is highly valued by farmers is soon clear on moving amongst them. Open boasting or denigration of rivals is rarely indulged in but they are keenly interested in the quality of each other's stock, constantly talking about it and eagerly noting improvements and deterioration in relative quality. The signs of this are the prices got for lambs and tups in the market and to a lesser extent prizes won at fairs and shows. (Farmers distinguish sharply between 'a good show beast' and beasts good for work and breeding. The two may coincide.) In most farmhouses photos of costly or prize winning animals hang on the wall, sometimes along with photos of the forbears of the farmer. One farmer was quite explicit on the matter, saying in the course of a conversation on local political office that it didn't matter much as he supposed that most farmers like himself wanted most to win a reputation as a good stocksman. Another sometimes used to boast to me a little in the maudlin stage of a drinking session, e.g., '. . . the top of the tree, that's it . . . mind you, you get no thanks for being at the top of the tree, oh no . . . people are jealous . . . just a lot of abuse. But I never mind them . . . I've been at the top of the tree for fifty years now and I've had my day . . The name of (my farm) has always stood for the best. The top of the tree. . . '

In wanting to be at the top of the tree farmers are not thinking solely of the financial returns this position brings. If farmers were interested only in the amount of money they made, and accorded reputation on this basis, obviously, those with bigger farms would always have a bigger reputation than those with smaller. This is not the case. The owner of the smallest farm in

[1] This characteristic of British farmers has long been noted. See e.g. J. Caird, *The Landed Interest*, London, 1880, page 58, where, speaking of tenant farmers he notes, 'Many of them are men of liberal education, and some of these are found in most parishes and in every county. A spirit of emulation exists among them, elicited by county, provincial and national exhibitions of agricultural stock, and by a natural desire, in a country where everthing is open to comment, not to be behind their neighbour in the neatness, style, and success of their cultivation, or in the symmetry and condition of their live-stock.'

Westrigg is widely esteemed as a breeder of tups and is listened to with respect on the subject in any company.

Interest in reputation is most clearly seen in the matter of breeding tups. The majority breed and sell tups at the annual tup fair held in Craigton. It lasts two days and is spoken of as 'the highlight of the year'. On the first day the beasts are exhibited and three prizes awarded: the following day they are sold by public auction. The excitement and interest the fair arouses can be judged by the amount of ceremony accompanying it.

About three weeks beforehand farmers start visiting each other and inviting visits to 'view the tups'. This they do in the evenings dressed in clean non-working clothes. The animals are penned and visitors and host regard them closely sometimes for several hours pointing out their good points and discussing tups in general. If a visitor shows marked interest in one the host may ask the party in for a drink.

During this period dressing the tups becomes the most important job of the shepherd put in charge of them, or of the farmer himself. Dressing means deftly and fastidiously clipping the fleece in such a way (I was told) as to hide the animal's bad points and show off its good ones to the best advantage. Several hours a day are spent thus, sometimes a whole day at a stretch, with the farmer often standing by watching if he is not doing it himself. The evening before the show the tups have their faces washed then painted white; the fleece is usually lightly sprinkled with sheep-dip to give it a yellow bloom. The decoration is repeated the evening after the show so that they will be looking their best at the sale next day.

At the show, attended by thousands of farmers and shepherds the excitement is intense, the atmosphere like that of a big football match. The reputation to be won is no mere parish wonder: the most celebrated of the Westrigg stocksmen, for example, sells tups to farmers in several of the dominions. Ribbands are pinned on the prizewinning animals. The victors celebrate according to temperament. One year the first prize was won by a Westrigg man normally a temperate fellow, but that afternoon he was seen dancing gleefully at the smiddy with his friend the blacksmith. The children on prizewinning farms sometimes turn up at school with the ribbands, to the chagrin of the others.

At the sale the next day excitement is equally high. When an animal sells for a sum in the region of £1,000 people say that there must have been a conspiracy between the seller and his friends, whereby they keep up the bidding (for each of their entries) and later exchange money to equalize gains and losses. When it is pointed out that not much money is likely to be made in this way people reply that it's not money the conspirators want but the 'name'. The names become widely known as accounts of the show and sale are broadcast and printed in the national newspapers.

Rivalry within friendship is always difficult. Sometimes a farmer buys a friend's tup at the sale 'just for friendship', then gives his shepherd instructions to keep the beast locked up in a shed to ensure that it never breeds with his own stock. It will be sold at some lesser sale next year.

The men who work in the fields are under close supervision by the farmer whether or not he works alongside them. Normally they assemble in the steading every morning to be given orders about the day's work. The shepherds are in a different position, especially those on outlying hirstles: one, for example, reckons that he sees his farmer only about four times a year. Each shepherd is entirely responsible for his hirstle and guards his independence. Several remarked that if the farmer came 'nosing' round their hirstles they would leave as that would imply lack of trust. All the shepherds speak of 'my hirstle'. Farmers rarely nose, acknowledging that a shepherd who did not know his job better than the farmer does would not be worth employing. The shepherd is left very much to himself and so important is his moral character and skill for the efficient running of a sheep farm that all farmers say that the most decisive control they have over the process is 'hiring the right herd'. On certain occasions the shepherds on one farm co-operate, particularly at clipping, dipping, sortings and innoculations – about thirty days a year.

The shepherd's independence and responsibility is recognized in the higher wages he gets.[1] It is probably also evident in membership of the Agricultural Workers Union. Though I was not able to check records, I was told that other agricultural workers are more enthusiastic supporters of the union than are the shepherds. However the union includes shepherds; like other

[1] See table of wages, page 150.

unions it represents the interests of its occupational categories in opposition to those of their employers. Farmers openly express hostility to the union but at the same time often congratulate themselves that their relationship to their men is more harmonious than is the case in most industries. The truth in this latter view is considered below. For the moment, the existence of the workers' union and farmers' hostility to it indicates the opposition between farmer and farm worker.

Workmen often express the opposition openly, e.g., a shepherd noted for his skill and conscientiousness – 'Farmers are mean you know. They're always good at finding excuses for not paying you more than the minimum wage.' Another shepherd – 'There isn't a meaner lot than farmers.' An agricultural worker referring to farmers' complaints that men do not work hard enough now – 'they've only themselves to blame. Before the war they made us work hard enough for them.' This latter is a common theme in workers' discussions on farmers – '. . . it's not so bad now but before the war you daren't say a word or out you'd go, and you had to take what wages they offered or they told you if you weren't satisfied there were plenty others who would be.'

All the workers agree that farmers have to be a bit more careful how they treat workers now that their own position *vis-à-vis* farmers has improved since the war. The latter correspondingly think their position has worsened. Their most frequent complaint is that workmen do not work so hard and are less amenable to control, mainly, farmers think, because there are not enough of them; some occasionally remark that the best thing that could happen to the countryside would be large scale unemployment in the towns, then there would be plenty of cheap labour, etc.

The opposition between the two became more openly expressed when the public hall was declared too dangerous for dancing in and parishioners decided to build a new one. Workmen started grumbling that farmers were rich enough to donate the necessary sum and ought to do so 'because they make it out of us' as one said. One, when his farmer remarked that he had heard that the hall was unsafe replied: 'And if there's not another built soon there'll be nobody in Westrigg to work for the farms.' Everyone knew that this was a hint that if farmers didn't provide the money their labour difficulties would be increased by men leaving the parish for more attractive places (see Chapter VIII). Farmers were fully aware of workmen's attitudes and made remarks like this: 'These people want everthing done for them. We don't use the hall, it's only they who do. If they want a hall they should raise the money.'

The opposition between the two is also apparent from the fact that farmers all have theories about the best techniques for getting the men to work harder. 'The great thing', says one, 'is not to give the impression you are ordering them. The great thing is to do it as if you were asking them.' 'I think if you work with the men and show an interest in what they are doing they will work too', says another. A young farmer once contrasted in mime the position of his father and himself with regard to the men. He imitated his father stepping out the door in the morning, twisting his moustache and snorting, 'then there wasn't a workman to be seen. They had all fled to the fields and were working like slaves. You and I can't do that' (turning to another farmer) 'they don't take any notice of us.'

Despite opposition between the two categories, workmen and farmers often work harmoniously together. To understand this relations between the men must be clarified.

Rivalry among the men

Rivalry between the men on one farm is not much in evidence but is apparent between men of different farms and especially among shepherds. Interest in reputation is as keen among shepherds as among farmers. The standards by which they are judged are known to everyone and there is consensus both among farmers and shepherds as to the efficiency of shepherds in the parish. This was clear from judgments made in the course of conversation and also from a grading of shepherds on a three point scale which two shepherds and two farmers did for me. Their ratings agreed exactly.

A good shepherd is one who can control his dogs and so move the sheep without fuss, who can spot sickness in the flock before it becomes dangerous, who consistently does his hill round, who can shear neatly and in general who cares for his flock. One sign of a good shepherd is his being a 'good kenner', i.e., he can recognize each animal in his flock individually. Considering that a flock may be as many as 500, that every year one-sixth are sold and lambs retained to replace them, this is no mean feat.[1] The most convincing sign is if, on taking a new job, the market price of lambs on his hirstle goes up relative to the others. As his work is thus publicly inspected and judged the shepherd becomes known and his reputation spreads. Even the way a shepherd moves his animals round the ring at the auction mart tells his peers whether or not he is a good craftsman.

Shepherds on the same farm do not allow each other to 'trespass' on each other's hirstles. This they sometimes explain on the grounds of jealousy. At any rate they are quite clear about the rivalry among them, often using sporting metaphors to talk about it as for example one who pointed to a neighbour's hirstle while doing the hill round and exclaimed, 'there's the bugger who beat me in the League Table last year'. (His neighbour's lambs got top price, his own second top.) Rivalry in efficiency in one of their main skills has become institutionalized through sheepdog trials, a popular entertainment in country towns and at agricultural shows. At these, shepherds (and those farmers who have learned the art) compete before an audience and judges in skilful handling of dogs. The trials are of varying importance culminating in an International Sheepdog Trial with competitors from Scotland, England and Wales. The best became known to shepherds in all three countries.

The other workers are less publicly acclaimed in this sheep rearing country. Even in Westrigg, however, the relative efficiency of the other workers is noted and experts whether in herding or other work get the regard of their fellows, are listened to and asked for advice and are usually popular at social gatherings. On a large farm it is one of the experts who is given the coveted job of preparing the tups for the fair. Even workmen who are politically antagonistic to bosses and interpret the esteem given a good workman as a trick that employers have somehow played on workmen still desire the respect accorded good workmen. One noted Socialist used to grumble that 'a good workman's the character of a horse', yet, as a noted craftsman, always took it upon himself energetically to direct the more difficult operations of the labour team.

[1] See Appendix 1.

Reputation as a good workman enables a man to get the best jobs (however he may define them). One year a new shepherd came to X farm and on his hirstle there was an extra good crop of lambs. He was very excited before the sale and said: 'This sale means a lot to me 'cos the lambs'll get a good price. Then the farmers'll start asking each other 'who's herding at X now' and I'll get a name. Then I'll be able to pick the jobs I want.' The importance of this for relations between farmers and men is that a good job is defined as either a shepherd manager's or as a job on a farm run by a good farmer.

The preference for work with an efficient farmer is openly stated for these reasons: (i) that work is easier under a good farmer; (ii) that it is impossible to acquire a name for oneself under a poor farmer. The preference is not merely a matter of talk but is shown in the fact that men stay longer in the employ of a good farmer than a poor one. One of the most highly esteemed farmers is said by his men to be 'The meanest man in the parish' – yet they stay with him. A rival speaks of him thus: 'I can't understand these men. There's X (the highly esteemed farmer), he never pays his men a ha'penny more than the minimum yet they stay with him a lifetime.' The point is admitted by officials of the Farmers' Union: in a discussion on the present shortage of agricultural labour one remarked that it was difficult to estimate the real extent of the shortage since on the whole it was the more inefficient farmers who complained most about it.

Good workmen and good farmers tend to seek each other out; each helps to build the reputation of the other and on those farms on which the two are found each respects the other's skill. By virtue of the bond of mutual respect the efficient farmer and the efficient workman work harmoniously together. This personal bond endures along with the opposition between the two administrative categories 'farmer' and 'agricultural worker'. It is because the latter are abstract administrative categories whose opposition is fought out on a national level that on any one farm work relations can be harmonious.

The Forest

The two forests do not fit into this scheme of relationships; they are related to the farms only in that they offer alternative employment for farm workers, an alternative that seems to be becoming more attractive than farm work.

The forest is a unit in a large bureaucratic organization, the Forestry Commission, which appoints managers and foremen to each forest. They have to qualify for these posts by attending forestry school and passing examinations. The manager can hardly be said to employ the labourers in his forest. Their wage is the minimum laid down for General Agricultural Workers and he cannot offer more or any perquisites. Many of the men who work under him will have applied for the job to a higher official who details applicants to forests in his area. Despite this there is the same opposition between forestry labourer and forestry management as between farm worker and farmer.

One manager remarked: 'The workers here don't know what work is. They don't work nearly fast enough. They're a poor bunch.' The labourers, aware that the manager has no control over their wages, do not express their hostility in terms of wages but in terms of the amount of work demanded of them. Since it is not the manager himself who supervises their daily labour but foremen, their hostility is directed largely against these latter. It is expressed in numerous ways: in bickering with them over the amount of work allocated or done, in obeying their orders with the utmost slowness, and in constant vituperative gossip and jokes behind their backs. What the labourers say they object to most is the foreman giving them orders (though they know perfectly well these are the manager's orders relayed through the foreman) and 'always watching to see if you're working'. This resentment arises because, as one labourer put it, 'The foreman's just really a worker, but he's a boss man'.

The unfortunate position of the foreman is apparent also in social life outside work. 'Worker' and 'bosses' belong to different social classes, do not associate in friendships and cliques with each other, and find friends in their own class. The foreman does not clearly belong to either class, and several complained that the major drawback to Westrigg was that they had no friends there.

Except for the fact that farms and forests are 'small firms' the description so far might apply in many features to any industrial population, and it may be asked at this point how far the parish is a 'rural community': the term normally implies some sort of distinct unit with a social life of its own, an 'area of common life'. Naturally no absolute answer can be given to such a question, community is a matter of degree. It is certain, however, that in the last fifty years the rural community has been completely transformed. The following two chapters describe this transformation.

CHAPTER III

HISTORY OF THE PARISH (I)

THE parish in this history is the rural parish of the Scottish border, and Westrigg features in it only as a source of illustration. I have taken the turn of the century as the starting point because many informants – some native to the parish and some not – could clearly recall social life as it was at the time. I have also used official records of Westrigg and a neighbouring parish, and some standard secondary sources in reconstructing the social organization of the parish. The use of such varied sources makes for a certain ambiguity in that data concerning the parish as an administrative unit, for example, applies to all parishes, while data concerning forms of entertainment perhaps applies only to the informant's own parish. From such comparison as I was able to make however, I am satisfied that the organization and changes described in this and the next chapter apply to all parishes in the district.

Over the period considered the parish has become less and less a social unit possessing an independent existence of its own, and parishoners have been drawn increasingly into a wider network of contacts and relationships. At the same time configurations of relationships between persons and groups within the parish have altered. These relationships were of several kinds. There were those among parishioners as members of an administrative unit and a community, those which joined together members of families and those which joined together the personnel of farms, and finally those which both separated and united parishioners in a system of social class. As I have little information concerning the family sixty years ago, it is only incidentally considered in this history.

Formerly the parish was an administrative unit within the structure of the state, controlling in several ways the lives of those living within its boundaries. This control was effected through two institutions, the Parish Council and the School Board.[1]

The Parish Council instituted by the Local Government Act (Scotland) of 1894, was elected every three years by the heritors and ratepayers of the parish. The office bearers within it were a chairman, treasurer and clerk, the first two elected, the latter appointed by the Council and usually not an elected member. Usually too the clerk was the rate collector and Inspector of Poor in the parish, for which duties he was paid about £14 a year. The Council was incorporated under the name of the parish council of the parish with power to sue and be sued and had perpetual right of succession.

The Council levied within the parish a rate not exceeding sixpence in the pound.

The duties of the Council were mainly:

(1) To administer the Poor Law in the parish. This involved levying a rate upon parish ratepayers, deciding whether applicants for public relief came within the categories entitled to it, and deciding on the amount and kind of relief. A 'casual ward' was maintained, i.e. a building within which vagrants and sick parishioners unable to be cared for in a house were housed and fed.

(2) To provide places for the reception and temporary detention of children against whom offences had been or were believed to have been committed, to direct proceedings to be taken in regard to ill treatment and neglect of children and to pay the cost of such proceedings.

(3) To administer the registrations of births, marriages, deaths, vaccinations, etc.

(4) To administer in transfers of property held wholly or mainly for the benefit of the inhabitants of the parish.

Stated in this bald way the duties of the Parish Council seem unimportant and truly only of parochial interest. This is not the case. The Poor Law was an institution of the greatest significance at this time,[2] providing the only public provision against

[1] For more detailed information on local government in Scotland see Sir W. Whyte, *Local Government in Scotland*, Edinburgh, 1925.

[2] On the importance of the Poor Law after the industrial revolution see K. Polanyi, *Origins of Our Time*, Gollancz, 1945. For an assessment of its effectiveness at the turn of the century see S. and B. Webb, *The Break up of*

the miseries – hunger, exposure, etc. – of unemployment and destitution. From accounts parishioners give, the casual ward in Westrigg (and in surrounding parishes) was never empty. A lady who was partly in charge of it says, 'There was always somebody wanting a night's shelter and meal, tramps and wandering bodies, or maybe somebody in the parish, but mostly tramps.' Moreover, the significance of these provisions cannot simply be assessed by the amount of relief they afforded to actual persons in want, because any hired employee (and they constituted the majority of the parishioners) might find himself unemployed or disabled in some way, from sickness or accident or old age.

In Westrigg there were five councillors of whom one was invariably a minister; there was usually, though not invariably, one of the larger farmers and the other three were usually small farmers. There was one short departure from this normal composition when a joiner got elected on to the Council, but he resigned after attending only a few meetings. From 1897 until the abolition of the Parish Council, the clerk, rate collector and Inspector of Poor in Westrigg was the schoolmaster of the main school.

To the Council was brought information concerning those matters it was empowered to deal with, and in accordance with the information received, the Council acted. For example, at the meeting of 3 August 1895, 'Mr. X, one of the councillors, reported the case of Mrs. Z. who is at present ill with a young family of five. The Inspector was instructed to have the usual application form filled up and was authorized to pay aliment at the rate of 10s. per week as long as Mrs. Z. remained in her present invalid condition.' Or there is the case of Mistress Y. receiving 4s. weekly for many years, and also, on the recommendation of the M.O. a bottle of whisky a week. On 13 February 1904 is

---

the Poor Law, London, 1909. It is interesting that the Webbs, bent on changing the administration of the Poor Law, were hard put to it to find fault with its administration in Scotland. They remark (page 71) 'We have been impressed with the much greater approach in Scotland to identity of treatment of similar cases in the same parish, and of similar cases in different parishes. . . There is a much nearer approach to an accurate, impartial and even execution of the will of the elected representatives (than elsewhere).' The Webbs believed this was due to the greater power of the Inspector of Poor in Scotland and to the claimant for relief from a Parish Council having a right to appeal to higher authority.

the entry, 'The Inspector also stated that a report had reached him that Mistress Y. was spending 3s weekly on whisky. He on inquiry found this report correct, and had put a stop to it.' These instances illustrate the control exerted upon the individual from within the parish.

A more drastic example is shown in the following entry – 'Dr. X having got notice to attend the meeting was asked to vindicate his character and clear himself of the scandal in connection with Mrs. Y. or send in his resignation of the office of Medical Officer to the Parish Council of Westrigg within a week of the date, failing which he would be served with a formal dismissal.' The doctor resigned though 'protesting against the illegality and injustice of the Council's action'.[1]

The School Board was instituted by the Education (Scotland) Act of 1872. This act introduced a new conception of the duties of parents with regard to their children's education, making them responsible for ensuring that their children attended school from the age of five until thirteen (though the School Board could grant special exemption). The education of children became a matter of great import, and the Board was empowered to enforce attendance of children and to prosecute parents who disobeyed the new laws.

The number of members on a school board varied from five to fifteen, this being determined for each parish by the Board of Education, the national authority. The members were elected 'by owners or occupiers of lands or heritage of the annual value of not less than four pounds, situated within the parish'. The board was a body corporate, with right of perpetual succession and power to acquire and hold land for purposes of the Act. The school, the teacher's house and lands attached to these were vested in and under the management of the Board. It was empowered to enter into contracts for the erection, enlargement and maintenance of these. The Board administered a fund raised by a rate levied within the parish. The Board fixed fees for the school, appointed teachers and had power to dismiss teachers. The minister was invariably a member of the Board; normally one of the big local landowners, or his estate factor was on it, and three of the small farmers.

[1] I am greatly indebted to the County Clerk for access to the minute books of meetings of Parish Councils and School Boards in the county.

The Board did not hesitate to use its authority. Here is an extract of 2 November 1917 – 'The Clerk stated that Mr. X., for his child Peter, and Mr. Y., for his child William, had been summoned to attend this meeting for failing to secure the regular attendance of their respective children at school.' The parents explained why the children's attendance was so poor but the Board . . . 'on consideration of both cases were of opinion that the explanations given were not sufficient and did not satisfy the Board. The Board therefore granted an Attendance Order in both cases. The meeting directed the Clerk to transmit the necessary certificate signed by the chairman to Robert McGeorge, Solicitor, Broadfield, the person appointed by the School Board to prosecute in terms of the Education Acts.' On 14 November 1914 'the Clerk reported that as instructed by the Attendance Committee he had issued warnings to the parents of fourteen of the children named . . .' (for irregular attendance).

The responsibilities of the Board to parishioners was increased in 1908 by its being made responsible for medical inspection of children. It also sometimes provided financial assistance in cases of treatment arising from the inspection.

Children got little direct experience of the world outside the parish. The parish school was the only one most of them ever attended, and even before leaving school they had been inducted into the adult world of employment. The minute book shows that sometimes girls of twelve were excused attendance in order to enter domestic service. A frequent request asked of the Board was to excuse some of the boys during days when farm work was particularly intensive.

As soon as they left school the children started work, the girls as domestic servants and the boys on a farm. Mr. William Martin, an elderly shepherd, describes this:

'In those days the children left school at twelve. If the boys were not needed at home they were hired to another shepherd from the beginning of lambing until the beginning of November. They assisted with the lambing, the garden, and perhaps a part of the hill till the sheep were clipped. Then the hay; when the herd went to cut the hay the boy went to the hill to see that there were no sheep left on the top and they could watch from where they worked to see that they all went out again. If one was seen lying back the boy was sent to see what was wrong . . . when I started herding I was just like the other boys then. I began at twelve years of age but was needed at home so I started on half a hirstle of 35 score and when I was sixteen I got the full hirstle, which I herded for thirty years.'[1] Herds who began before 1939 give much the same account of their starting.

The changes which have occurred to the parish over the last fifty years are vividly exemplified in the changes in the role of the schoolmaster, for whereas he was formerly a person of note in the parish, with a large measure of independence in performing his job of educating the parish children, he now has no power in the parish and in the performance of his job merely carries out instructions given him by an agency outside the parish.

The schoolmaster had much more control over school affairs than he has now. He made his own programme of instruction, though of course reading, writing and arithmetic were the main subjects taught. Natives of Westrigg (of forty and above) recall with glee how their dominie, who was very fond of curling, used to close the school for a week or more when the season was on, or how in later life, when he had a car, he would occasionally close the school for a day while he went off to Broadfield.

The schoolmaster was usually a powerful figure in the parish When the Westrigg dominie first arrived in the parish in 1897 he was straightway appointed Clerk of the Council and Inspector of Poor. These, with the position of assistant Registrar (and Librarian if there was a library) seem to have been regarded as the normal perquisites of the schoolmaster.

Not only did the schoolmaster wield power in these official capacities, but in an unofficial way he was a leading figure in the parish. Farmers came to him to have their accounts checked and to ask his advice on how to keep them. Any of the labouring population who had to deal with official bodies both inside and outside the parish came to him for an interpretation of laws and regulations and advice on how to approach the authorities.

Not only was the Parish a local political unit, it was also a community within which by far the greater part of the individual's social and economic relationships were found. Or

[1] Mr W. Martin, 'Experiences in herding Cheviot Hill Sheep during the last Sixty Years', pages 14–16 in *Hill Sheep Husbandry in the Scottish Border*, being the proceedings of a Conference of Farmers held in the Tait Hall, Kelso, 8th January 1952.

rather, his relations outside the parish were fewer than they are now.

The roads into the two towns were unsurfaced. Sometimes, in flood, sections would be washed away. All farmers then had horse-drawn carriages, but the majority of the rest of the population had to walk if they wished to visit a town. There were two public means of transport. One was the postmaster's cart which he drove to and from Broadfield daily except Sunday; for a few pence he would take a passenger. Those who remember him say he 'took so long you were quicker walking'. The other was a horse-drawn bus owned by a Craigton firm which operated on some market days between Craigton and Westrigg.

Though it was possible to get to town on these vehicles or by walking, hours of work were long and money wages low, so that few people had either the time to spare for a visit or money to spend when they got there. The shepherds and cattlemen who drove their animals to market might spend the rest of the day in town when the market was over, but this was the only regular visiting of the town there was. It was especially difficult for wives and mothers to get to town and they very rarely did so. Even the men now when discussing the past usually add, that as one said, 'It was hardest on the women then, and it's them I pity', because they so rarely got away from the parish. Informants who remember the days when a visit to town was 'a rarity' include not only the middle aged and the elderly but also men and women in their thirties. As one of these latter said, 'When I was a bairn I hardly knew what a shop was, I'd only been to town once or twice till after I started working.'

As for 'commercial transport', the only regular vehicle was again the postmaster's cart. Small goods could be sent up by it from town. There were no town shopkeepers making regular trips into the parish as there are now.

There operated within the parish then an exchange of services which has since been greatly reduced, for there were at that time several tradesmen in the parish who have either disappeared or who can no longer supply the sort of services parishioners now require. These were the blacksmith (also wheelwright), the miller, the bootmaker, the tailor and the joiner. The blacksmith and his assistant repaired all farm machinery, carts and carriages, shoed the horses, and also themselves

45

fashioned many of the smaller farm implements – spades, hoes, etc. There was a mill in Westrigg then (and in most of the surrounding parishes) grinding locally grown grain and the meal produced was consumed within the parish.

The parish also supported a full time bootmaker who fashioned boots as well as repairing them. In those days farm workers who wore boots bought in a shop in town were laughed at by the rest. The ones made by the local bootmaker were 'more comfortable anyway' as one shepherd said. The tailor had four journeymen working for him who walked the surrounding countryside with samples of cloth, took orders for suits and dresses, and returned to the shop in Westrigg to make them.

A sketch of 'standards of living' of fifty years ago confirms the picture so far presented of a fairly high degree of economic self-sufficiency in the parish, or at any rate a higher degree than obtains now. For nearly all the food eaten was produced in the parish itself. Apart from tradesmen, two or three retainers of the Duke of Garvel, the minister and the schoolmaster, everyone in the parish was attached to a farm. Money wages did not exceed about thirty-two pounds per year, and the rest of the wage consisted of farm produce. Maidservants and many of the unmarried male employees received their meals from the farm kitchen. Every family kept chickens and many a cow, while most cultivated a garden of vegetables. Many reared a pig or two every year to supply themselves with bacon. Sheep which died on the hill from accident or disease were eaten provided the carcase was discovered before putrefacation set in. The only items of food which were regularly imported into the parish were sugar, tea and flour. It was the custom in many households to lay in a store of these twice a year.

Standards of food consumption may be judged from descriptions like the following. A fifty-year old farmer recalls his boyhood. 'Livin' was a lot rougher then. You had porridge twice a day, and you used to eat a lot of broth and tatties – there was always plenty of meat, mind you. I've eaten a lot of braxy[1] sheep myself. I used to think fried mutton was good but I had some recently and didn't like it. Oh but it was rough then – no fancy cakes then for your tea, just scones and tea.' He was a farmer's son, and probably had a higher standing of living than

[1] Braxy – a disease which used to kill a great many sheep, rare now.

the majority of parishioners. An elderly ploughman recalls his first job as a boy 'the first job I had was at £5 for six months, an' I believe I had to work harder for that than I've ever done since. I slept in a loft and I was fed on porridge and milk and tatties and I got tea on Sundays.'

At that time peat and wood were the only fuels used by the majority of the population and both were got in the parish.

Every shepherd then was entitled to 'one fat sheep' per year, i.e., a sheep from his master's flock which he himself chose. The meat was eaten while from the fat was made candles and tallow for greasing his boots. The skin was made into rugs or sold. So frugal were people then that shepherds while walking the hills in the course of their daily work used to gather up the 'pooks' (i.e., wisps of wool) that the animals shed and store them. In two or three years they had several pounds of wool, which they took to Broadfield mills and either sold or had made into several yards of worsted. Once in conversation with a shepherd we talked about fishing, then about the 'pack' (see page 53). He told me how one year his total income from the pack was £9, and added 'fishing – in those days you had to fish to live.' Stories are still told in the parish of families so short of food that they would eat sea trout after they had spawned, a condition in which they are apparently unpalatable for most.

The relative independence of the parish from outside contacts had its counterpart in an internal self-sufficiency and intensity of social relations. These cannot be analysed with sociological accuracy now, since information about them can be got only from the elderly who speak in sweeping generalities. When talking spontaneously of the past they nearly always start with accounts of 'entertainment', and always stress that (apart from men drinking on market days) they did not seek entertainment in local towns.

The only recreational institution which met regularly seems to have been the men's bowling club. People recall when there were only two dances a year, a concert or two and a whist-drive. This does not mean that this was all the organized entertainment open to parishioners, for in those days it was considered 'nothing' to walk ten miles after work to attend a dance in another parish. However, the low value placed on organized entertainment in the parish is seen in the fact that there was no special building devoted to it. Dances and whist-drives were held either in the school or in some barn. It was not until 1922 that a public hall was erected in the parish.

At this time however there was a great deal more informal entertainment within the parish than there is now. Parishioners visited each other more. On these visits they might play cards or perform with musical instruments or simply talk. There were other ways in which they entertained themselves too. The elderly recall seeing 'thirty or forty boys and girls dancing on the road outside the smiddy on a summer evening', for example. The middle aged recall with delight the ploys they used to get up to as youths – unhinging gates and hiding them on the hillside, spreading tar on the handles of implements and so on. The youths had a way of dealing with an unpopular adult then – they would tar his cow or pig and turn it loose so that he became covered with tar recapturing it.[1] They would engage in trials of strength at the smiddy. The blacksmith, who thinks that the erection of the public hall in 1922 did 'a lot of good for the parish' because it provided a place where the youths could bowl twice a week 'instead of raising mischief', yet has an ambivalent attitude about it. He also remarks that there doesn't seem to be 'as much life about the place' as there used to be when the youths raised mischief.

In work-a-day activities too, parishioners entered into relationships with each other much more than they do now. Mutual aid was more frequent among neighbours than is the case now. Occasions specially mentioned for this were peat cutting, blanket washing and wall papering – but they say 'There didn't have to be any set occasion – if someone in the house was ill, or if you were doing any big job, your neighbours would be in asking if you wanted a hand. Then sometimes later you would give them a hand at something.' It is impossible to assess just how much of this sort of mutual aid there was as compared with the present day. There is however one institutionalized form which has disappeared altogether, a form which does indicate how

---

[1] This type of 'youth culture' in which the normal ebullience of youth serves the older generation, in which youth provides the sanctions for the norms of adult culture, is described by Rees in his book mentioned above. It is probably an essential feature of any community which is well integrated mainly along kinship lines.

much the parish formed a distinct social unit. This was the 'clipping band'.

The clipping band was composed of all the shepherds in the parish, and most of the farmers too. Each year at clipping time (early July) the band went round every farm and clipped all the sheep. The order in which they visited farms was fixed by tradition and never varied. It was the duty of the farmer to feed the band every day it worked on his farm. The band seems at first sight to be merely a rational organization of labour for getting work done quickly. There were however ceremonial elements in it which clearly show that it was not merely a rational organization of labour, but had the nature of a ritual expressing the unity of the parish. Apart from the communal meals eaten throughout the day, the men did not turn up in their dirtiest working clothes, as one would expect for a job like sheep shearing but in newly cleaned clothes. Often at the end of a day's clipping there would be impromptu fiddling, singing and dancing. There was always festivity of some sort after the last day's clipping. If the band had been only a way of getting work done there seems no reason for it to have disappeared, for sheep still have to be clipped. If however it is regarded as a ceremony expressing the unity of the parish, then its disappearance becomes at once understandable. For it is to be expected that as the parish lost its unity, ceremonies expressing that unity would disappear.

Finally, the elderly say that simply to live in the parish formerly meant that a person was an object of interest to all other parishioners. Every adult knew of the existence of everyone else, could name them and recognize them. The important events in an individual's life – birth, christening, marriage and death – were announced in church, and as everyone went to church everyone knew of them. A newcomer to the parish was semi-officially welcomed into it by a minister, who had to be the first person to visit the newcomer.

The history of the Church in the local community in Scotland is too complex a subject to be treated in detail here.[1] Many

[1] There is an extensive literature touching on this subject, though few of the works deal with it from a sociological point of view. Three recent and relevant books are, G. D. Henderson, *The Claims of the Church of Scotland*, London, 1951; Augustus Muir, *John White*, London, 1958; John Highet, *The Scottish Churches*, London, 1960.

parishes (like Westrigg) had two congregations, of the Church of Scotland and of the Free Church. In some parts of the country which relied a great deal on casual seasonal labour, in which farm servants were accustomed to change their place of work almost annually, this floating population seems to have taken no part in Church affairs. In some districts there were anti-Church movements among the working class. However, this does not seem to have been the case in Border districts, and from accounts parishioners give only the very old and the sick did not appear in Church on Sunday, the rest walking up to six miles to attend. The social organization of the parish was displayed in the seating arrangements in the main church. A number of pews were reserved for the Duke of Garvel and his household who owned most of the land and had a shooting lodge in the parish in which he sometimes resided. No one else could use these pews so that even in the Duke's absence Garvel was always present. Heritors (owners of taxable property) similarly had their own pews, inherited by a man's heirs along with his property. Other people may have occupied some customary place in some pew but the pew was not named after them, as were the heritors' and the Duke's. Whole families attended church together, and maid-servants usually dressed in some distinctive uniform sat in the same pew as the families employing them.

The Kirk Session (the body administering the affairs of a congregation) is composed of the minister and elders elected from the congregation by the congregation. Fifty years ago most parishioners considered it an honour to be elected an elder. The minister was regarded with the utmost respect and could privately rebuke persons for lapses of piety. As one old far-mer put it 'he was a power in the land second to the Duke.' It is important to note that the office of minister was the object of this respect, not the persons occupying the office at any given time. People yet under forty recall how when they were children they were sent out of the house by the backdoor when the minister was seen approaching the front door on one of his visits, their parents terrified lest they would do or say something to affront this powerful person.

The minister had a great deal of secular power too, as we saw from his membership of the Parish Council and the School Board. In the course of his duties he played an important part in integrating the parish. He was the only person who had the right to enter every household, and in doing so he kept everyone informed of events in the parish, and passed judgment on them. When a newcomer entered the parish he had to visit him, formally welcome him into the congregation and inform him about local affairs.

The Sabbath was then truly a holy day during which taboos were laid upon many of the weekday profane activities, taboos which impressed the sacredness of the day upon all. Everyone wore special clothes and refrained from gainful work. In some households no cooking was done. A somewhat extreme case of ritualization of behaviour was that of a minister who would not let his chickens out of the coop on Sunday lest he profane the sacred day.

Fifty years ago all but three farms in Westrigg were owned by the Duke of Garvel and leased to tenants. The landlord played an active part in farming, being responsible for half the cost of any improvements to the farm. The better off the farm, the higher the rent he could charge. He could terminate the lease of any farmer whom he thought was ruining the farm.

Through this power he had over the farmers the Duke wielded considerable influence in local affairs. So at any rate people say, though informants could never give instances of what exactly they meant by saying that 'the Duke was the law up here'; or as one put it 'he strode like a lion through the place.' Probably what is meant by these sort of statements is simply that all parishioners were awed at the power and wealth and rank of the Garvels and carried out any commands he cared to give.

The farm formed a small group within which the individual lived the greater part of his or her life. The personnel of the farm consisted of the farmer (i.e., the person paying rent to the Duke or the person owning the farm) and his family, and the persons (with their families) employed by him to perform the work required on the farm.

The majority of the population then as now consisted of employees (and their families) of the farmers. Both male and female employees at this time were called 'farm servants'. The girls, housemaids and milkmaids, normally came from one of the farm servants' families resident in the parish, or if not in

Westrigg then in one of the adjoining parishes. The hiring and supervision of these girls was done by the farmer's wife who usually knew, by repute at least, both the girl and her family. Often in fact the mistress in need of a maid would ask a particular girl who had taken her fancy to come and work as a maid for her.

Male farm servants were hired at Hiring Fairs, held once or twice yearly on fixed dates in various country towns. Farm servants seeking employment congregated in one of the main streets of the town; farmers seeking labour strolled through the crowd picking out likely looking men and youths, or men whom they already knew to be good workmen. Having picked someone, the farmer sought to 'make a bargain' with the servant. The conditions of farming and the quantity of labour available set limits to the variability of the terms arrived at, but each bargain arrived at was unique and differed in its terms from every other bargain.

The bargain consisted of two parts, money wages and 'perquisites'. A shepherd's money wage was around £30 per year, and a ploughman's (in this district) two to four pounds less than a herd's. However, cash formed only a part of the bargain, the rest consisting of farm produce and various rights described below. This other part of the total wage is nowadays often called 'perquisites', suggesting that these are an addition to the money wage – a sort of free gift from generous farmers to employees. In point of fact 'perquisites' were a customary part of the total payment from farmer to servant, and the servant depended upon 'perquisites' to sustain him and his family almost as much as he did upon his cash wage. The following scale seems to have been general in Westrigg for a married herd.

(1) A cottage to house himself and his family. A few shillings rent could be charged by the farmer for this. However, many cottages then, as now, were rent free.
(2) Sixty-five stone of meal per year. Sixty stone of this was for consumption by the herd and family, and five was for making gruel fed to sick sheep at lambing time.
(3) From five to 10 cwt. of potatoes.
(4) A supply of peats for fuel. Generally there was no limitation placed on the amount – each simply cut sufficient to last his household for a year.

(5) 'One fat sheep' per year. The shepherd chose one sheep from his masters' flock to be disposed of as he thought fit (see page 47).

(6) Up to three pints of milk a day, or 'the keep of a cow'.

The list was much the same for other categories of servants except for the fat sheep, which was solely a shepherd's perquisite. In general too, only shepherds had the right to the keep of a cow, the other servants receiving three pints of milk a day.

Hours of work did not form a subject for bargaining: they were decided solely by the will of the farmer – men had to work as long as he commanded them to or be fired. As an elderly ploughman put it 'You were waked up at five in the morning and you worked on till you were told to stop in the evening.' Often in summer months men worked on till darkness 'worried to death with midges and fair dropping with hunger. Oh it wasn't like it is now – soon as five o'clock comes he's (i.e., the farmer nowadays) ordering you out the field as fast as you can get – he doesn't want to pay overtime.' This power that the farmer had did not mean that the farm servant worked every day from dawn till dusk, for just as work went on in summer as long as the weather was good, so when it rained work stopped, and in winter the men often spent days sitting in a barn or hayshed, talking and playing cards.

Holidays too did not form a subject for bargaining. There were no statutory holidays such as are laid down by Wages Boards now. There were only three customary holidays in the year – New Year's Day and the two Hiring Fair days.

One very important variation in this general account of the bargain must be noted, a variation which concerned a whole category of farm servants, viz. the shepherd. Up till about forty years ago the majority of herds did not receive any cash in the payment made to them by the farmer. Instead, each herd owned a 'pack' of sheep of his own, and the right to graze it on the master's land constituted his 'wages'. As with other details of the relation between master and servant there were customary rules concerning the constitution of the pack. It consisted of 36 breeding ewes and 9 hogs and was then valued at about £100. From the sale of lambs, wool, and cast sheep the herd made a yearly income. It is impossible to say what the income from a pack was since it varied from year to year with the market price of lambs, etc., with vicissitudes of weather, and from farm to farm with the quality of the stock and the herbage. In a bad snowstorm a herd might lose all his pack.

Owning a pack made the shepherd, as one said, 'a bit of a farmer in a small way' and distinguished him from other farm workers. He was treated rather more respectfully by the farmer, and it seems that some shepherds 'thought themselves above the others' and refused to associate with them.

Firing, just as much as hiring, was regulated by customary rules. In this district the summer hiring fair was held on the last day of May. Six months later came 'the speaking time'. The farmer had to approach the servant and in an indirect way the two either reaffirmed the bargain of the previous May or agreed to dissolve it. Normally speaking time was considered a delicate matter, since one of the two might unwittingly give offence to the other. A suggestion by the farmer that the servant might want to leave might be interpreted by the servant that the farmer was suggesting that he ought to leave.

Once the bargain had been made the farmer was 'the master' who had at his disposal the time and labour of the 'servant' to a degree unimaginable today. The farm servant's life was almost wholly enclosed in his relation to the farm. Not only was his time and labour so much at the disposal of the farmer but he depended for his sustenance largely upon farm produce paid to him by the farmer. Further details indicate how clearly the farm servant and his family were tied to the farm.

Quite apart from perquisites the servant ate a great many meals provided by the farmer and his wife. The farmer had customary obligations to provide these, the most important occasions being at clipping, dipping, harvesting, haymaking and threshing. These meals were sometimes eaten outside in the fields but just as often were eaten in the farmhouse kitchen. Estimates of the amount of meals supplied per year vary from 25-40 days' meals per year – we may say that for the equivalent of a month a year the servant ate at the expense of the farmer and his wife.

Maids and some of the unmarried male servants were even more closely attached to the farmhouse. Maids were part of the household in the sense that they lived in the farmhouse and ate all their meals in the farm kitchen. Part of the bargain between mistress and maid was often that the mistress had to supply the maid with one new dress every year. Indeed, an outfit of clothes, free meals and lodging, was often the whole bargain when a girl first entered into service. In this case the mistress as a reward might give the girl a few shillings to attend some local fair once a year. Often unmarried male servants and especially boys were included not perhaps in the household but among the more valuable stock in the steading. They would sleep in a loft above the horses and be fed from the farmhouse.

The farm servant's family were incorporated into the farm in various ways. Very often a man and wife would be hired together, the wife as a sort of part-time maid to help with the milking. Even when this was not the case the farm servant's family was often incorporated into the labour team. At haymaking and harvesting in particular, women and children all helped in the fields and were recompensed by sharing in the communal meal distributed by the farmer. At peat digging too wives and children went out with the men and helped. Babies on these occasions were left in a corner of a field 'happed in a plad' as the elderly ladies say.

Schoolgirls in a farm servant's family helped their mothers in their own house. Boys, especially shepherds' sons, were inducted into the adult labour team long before they left school through having to help their fathers during holidays and after school hours. Shepherds' sons even while still at school had to help their fathers at lambing time and clipping. A herd aged 35 says of the clipping bands: 'When I started twenty years ago it was nearly all stool clipping then, and we boys had to do the catching (of the sheep) and we had to lift it up on to the stool for them, they never thought of giving you a hand up.' In other words the boys had a definite task to do. In fact all shepherds' sons learned the craft from their fathers long before they left school so that as soon as they left they were able to begin employment as assistant herds, or 'boys'.

At the time of which we are speaking a farmer and his family were as much a part of the labour team as the servant and his family. This may seem so obvious as to be hardly worth mentioning, but in point of fact it stands in marked contrast to the state of affairs today, where on some farms not only does the farmer's family take little or no part in the work of the farm, but the farmer himself stands aloof from work in the sense of manual labour, and contents himself with supervising the work of the men. A local phrase describes aptly the relation of these latter to the labour team; it is said of them that 'they never have their jackets off from one day to the next.' Fifty years ago this was most unusual. All took part in the everyday work on the farm in addition to supervising the work of their servants. Many farmers learned to herd and could do the work of any herd who fell ill. Similarly, their wives and children were also to some extent part of the labour team. All farmers' wives could milk, make butter, etc., and though these jobs were not part of the daily routine for them all they 'thought nothing' of doing them. Many of the farmers' children went to the local school and helped on the farm after school hours and during holidays.

The local class system at this time can only be described in general terms. The following sketch is partly an historical reconstruction from accounts of it given by elderly parishioners and partly an inference from my analysis of it at the present time (see Chapter V). The class of highest prestige was 'the county', owners of large tracts of land and persons with hereditary titles and their near relatives. One such family owned most of the farms in the parish. The next class consisted of tenants and owners of the larger farms along with the minister; the next of the smaller farmers with the schoolmaster and perhaps a few of the more prosperous tradesmen. Below them came the majority of the population: farm servants and tradesmen. Finally, a class that has all but disappeared was composed of tramps and also of a few individuals (and occasionally families) in habitual receipt of Poor Relief.

The difference between the majority of the labouring population and this lowest class seems to have been that the labourers had steady jobs, lived in cottages and accepted normal standards of personal cleanliness, whereas the lowest class were shiftless, constantly on the move and unclean in their personal habits. Since its members were constantly on the move its composition in any one parish was constantly changing, yet as an element of the population it seems always to have been there.

It is apparent that this class system represented a hierarchy of economic power, those of a higher class having power over those of a lower, either through owning land and hence having power over tenants, or through owning or leasing farms and having power over the labouring population.

There was the same unequal distribution of local political power among the classes. It has already been mentioned that the Parish Council of Westrigg consisted throughout its history (with the sole and temporary exception of the joiner) of farmers and the minister, and that its clerk and Inspector of Poor was the school-master. Accordingly, not only did the two classes represented on the council control the lives of the labouring population from day-to-day in their capacity of employers, but when one of the labouring population fell destitute (which in practice meant that no one would employ him or her) these two classes decided whether or not the pauper was entitled to relief and to how much. Their control over the labouring population was complete.

Judging from informants' accounts, attitudes of deference were more publicly displayed than they are now. Deference behaviour was more constantly and strictly demanded of the labouring classes by the two farming classes, in the form of cap-lifting and 'sir-ing'. As the blacksmith said, 'It used to be terrible, always lifting up your bonnet, you barely had your bonnet on all bloody day'. A farm servant who neglected to give these signs of his position to any in the class above risked being branded as 'impudent' and fired from his job. As there was never any shortage of labour farmers had no hesitation in firing them.

In many respects the county was utterly different in culture from the other classes. Whether as scholars and patrons of the arts or as devotees of the pleasures of hunting and opulent hospitality they moved in realms the others might admire but not enter. They were not confined to a narrow locality in their contacts; their culture conformed to standards which applied to their counterparts throughout Europe. It would be wrong however to suggest that their links with the classes below were solely predatory. They shared with them interests in efficient husbandry and stockbreeding, and an understanding of rural life and work. Some parishioners maintain that leased farms on a large estate always were and still are in better condition than those which are owner-occupied. I have also heard farmers say that the economic advantages of leasing (see page 51) outweigh any alleged benefits of owning.

Among the three remaining classes – those forming the bulk of the population – large and small farmers and the farm servants, there were differences in 'standards of living' between the two farming classes and the rest. The standard of living in the parish fifty years ago already described above (p. 46f.) was that of the majority of the population, the farm servants and their families; that of the farming and professional classes was very much higher. The two farming classes lived in larger and more spacious houses, wore clothes of better quality than the labourers, and never had to depend on fishing the burns to get something to eat. Each family in the former two classes had its horse carriage, so that they could more easily leave the parish for visits to town.

Apart from those items which are normally included in the notion of a 'standard of living' however, there seems to have been more cultural uniformity among these classes than there is now. This perhaps resulted from the majority of the persons in these classes receiving the same education from the same two agencies, the parish school and the Kirk. Probably, too, the fact that the whole population worked provided a basic culture for everyone.

From all accounts there were no great differences in culture in the ordinary sense. The Bible and Burns were the staple reading matter of all classes, and Scottish dance music and song the only music there was. All classes spoke much the same dialect, as the speech of the two farming classes was not so anglicized as it is now.

CHAPTER IV

HISTORY OF THE PARISH (II)

THE account of the parish in the last chapter has perhaps made it appear to have been a completely self-contained group. This of course was not the case; it was a unit of local government in a framework established by the State, and the authority of the Parish Council and the School Board derived from it. Economically the parish was a small area of production subject to the forces of a world-wide market. The stock bred there was sold to buyers in various places in Britain and much of the wool cropped was eventually exported to Italy. Returns from farming here as in the rest of the country depended on production and conditions in other parts of the world, particularly America and Australia. Emigration abroad or to towns in Britain had already been standard practice (though to what extent I do not know; see page 139) for several generations. Yet though parishioners were involved in a network of relations extending beyond the parish boundaries, their everyday social environment was provided by family and farm and the relatively contained network of parochial relationships. Since 1900, however, events and policies originating outside have abolished the parish as an administrative unit and destroyed the relative containedness of the local network. Relationships between employer and employee have been considerably altered. Parishioners have been drawn into a wider dispersed network stretching beyond the parish, and their relations within the parish have altered accordingly.

A detailed account of these events lies outside the scope of this study. I shall merely sketch in the main ones and consider their effect upon the parish.[1] The first was a reorganization of parts of

[1] For this chapter I found the following most useful, R. C. K. Ensor, *England, 1870–1914*, O.U.P., 1930. Trevelyan, *British History in the Nineteenth Century*, London, 1922. T. H. Marshall, *Citizenship and Social Class*, Cambridge, 1950.

the State administrative apparatus; broadly, those concerned with local government and the welfare of the individual citizen. It has been lucidly analysed by T. H. Marshall and I can do no better than paraphrase some of his main points.[1] It consisted in a concentration of function in a few organs of administration – Ministries and County Councils – simultaneously with an enlargement of the lowest level of territorial unit served by those agencies (or district branches of them).

The major changes in local government which have affected the parish since 1900 were effected by the Local Government (Scotland) Act of 1929 and the Education (Scotland) Acts of 1918 and 1929. By the first of these the Parish Council was abolished and its main functions transferred to the County Council (or to Town Councils in large burghs). Each parish now elects one or, in some cases, two Councillors to the County Council, but here the parish is merely an electoral division and its councillor is responsible to the electorate of the County as a whole along with the other Councillors. The parish as a unit of Local Government only exists now for the registration of birth marriage and death.

Various Education Acts have been equally destructive of the administrative autonomy of the parish, the most important being the Act of 1918. By this, the unit of administration in education was changed from the parish to the County through the abolition of the School Board and the institution of Education Authorities for each county. By an Act of 1928 the functions of these Authorities were vested in the County Council.

Guiding the process sketched in above was a new conception of the rights of the citizen, rights to a guaranteed minimum of means of subsistence, health and education. The Poor Law in the form described on pages 40-41 had been in operation since 1834. Increasing numbers of paupers and movements of population throughout the nineteenth century rendered its provisions increasingly inadequate and its application cumbersome. Practical steps to reform it began in 1909 with the inauguration of the old age pension scheme, followed in 1911 with the first unemployment insurance scheme. In 1918 the disability of disenfranchisement was removed from receipt of poor relief. The original unemployment insurance scheme has since been gradu-

[1] T. H. Marshall, *op. cit.*

ally extended in scope both as regards the population served and the kinds of services offered until now it is a vast scheme to insure the whole population of Britain against sickness, disability and unemployment.[1]

Another equally important process has been the formation and growth of a nation-wide association, the Farm Servants' Union, which has broken the bonds that joined the farm servant so closely to his farm. Farmers also formed a union and official representatives to these two bodies now regulate the relationship between all farmers and farm servants. Latterly the State has intervened in bargaining between the two unions.

Scottish farm servants were slow to form a trade union.[2] In England a flourishing Union of Agricultural Workers was founded in 1872, the aim of which in the words of its founder Joseph Arch was 'to raise wages, shorten the hours, and make a man out of a land-tied slave.'[3] Though the Scottish farm servant was just as much a 'land-tied slave' as his English counterpart, he never seems to have made any serious attempt to alter his position during the nineteenth century.

In 1912, however, Scottish farm servants founded a union with the same general aims as those announced by Arch. The union was nation wide and linked farm servants in all parts of the country in an association to prosecute those aims. The method officers used was to persuade farm servants at hiring fairs to demand a certain wage and to refuse a bargain in which the wage offered fell below that. Thus each servant no longer bargained alone but only as a representative of his occupational category and knowing that many others in his occupation were supporting him in his claims. By these means farm servants managed to increase their wages by a few shillings a week, and to get a half day's holiday every Saturday. In 1917 farmers formed a union and for some time afterwards officials of the two unions bargained over wages on behalf of all farmers and all servants.

After the First World War the agricultural industry entered another long depression and the Farm Servants Union made little headway with its aims. In 1932 it became affiliated to a

[1] This is practically a quotation from T. H. Marshall, *op. cit.*
[2] T. Johnstone, *History of the Working Class in Scotland*, Glasgow, 1929.
[3] R. Groves, *Sharpen the Sickle*, 1952.

more powerful union, the Transport and General Workers, and soon after this it began to demand wage increases and shorter working hours. A new feature of its demands was for a legally guaranteed minimum wage. This could of course only be guaranteed by the State, and from that time on the State has intervened in the regulation of the relationship between farmer and farm servant. An Agricultural Wages Board for Scotland was instituted composed of an equal number of representatives from the two unions, two members appointed by the Department of Agriculture for Scotland, and an independent chairman. The history of negotiations over wages and working hours does not concern us; here the main point is that the farmer and the farm servant are no longer directly related to each other as formerly but are related to each other as members of two associations, membership of which is nation wide. The Wages Board's decisions regarding payment and working hours are binding upon all persons in the two occupational categories, whether or not they are actual members of the Unions. It is also of course relevant to this account of the recent history of the parish that money wages for agricultural workers have increased considerably during this period (se epage 150 for scale). To what extent, however, this has been due to union activity and to what extent to increased productivity of farms through new techniques or to state subsidies to farmers is a large question, which is irrelevant to my theme. A daily stint of so many hours per day, varying with seasons, has been established for farm labour (except shepherds, see page 150). Whether this has shortened the working hours of the farm labourer over the course of a year is questionable, but by general consent of farm workers it has eased their lot considerably.

Another process of great importance has been the development of systems of public transport. Buses replaced horse-drawn carts, roads were improved and regular and frequent communication with neighbouring towns became the norm. A bus carries mail between Broadfield and Westrigg twice daily and can be used by the public. Another bus takes the older schoolchildren to a school in Broadfield and the unmarried girls to work in Broadfield tweed mills. On Saturdays a bus runs two trips into Craigton. Parishioners can visit towns with ease while increased money wages and leisure hours provide incentive to do so.

At the same time, town tradesmen are enabled to bring their goods into the parish. The basic timetable of tradesmen's visits is as follows:

Day	Type	From
Tuesday	Grocer and Baker	Broadfield
Wednesday	Butcher, Grocer,	Craigton, Craigton
	Fruit & Vegetable	Broadfield
Thursday	Grocer	Broadfield
	Butcher	Craigton
Friday	Grocer, Baker	Broadfield

These are routine visits; the parishioners depend on the tradesmen coming on these days for their weekly supplies of food. In addition, goods supplied in bulk are brought into the parish as occasion demands; for example, meal and fodder for animals are brought in from various places, and a Broadfield firm delivers coal which almost everyone now uses to some extent.

One other process which must be mentioned is the great expansion of industries producing 'consumer goods' of all sorts since the last decade of the nineteenth century, goods ranging from ready-made horseshoes to corn flakes, from suits of clothing to wireless sets.

These events already describe the gradual disappearance of what was once an important social unit, the country parish. Rights, which an individual once possessed by virtue of his membership of this unit, he now possesses by virtue of his membership of either the County or the State. It is now the duty of the County to educate him, for instance, and the duty of the State to aliment him should he lose his job. And just as these rights now accrue to the individual by virtue of his membership of a larger social unit than the parish, so his social contacts have widened. He is no longer so dependent on other members of the parish economically nor for recreation. His rights and obligations as regards employment are no longer arranged between his employer and himself. Even the social horizon of the children has been enormously widened by their being sent to schools in town after the age of thirteen. In short, the term 'parish' now refers merely to a population living within a geographically defined boundary which has little sociological significance.

I shall now describe the effects of these events and processes in the parish. Since it is simply no longer a unit of local government (except for registration purposes) there is little to be said on this score. The abolition of the Parish Council however did mean a weakening of the local power of the two classes whose representatives sat on it. This is discussed on page 73. Here I shall consider the effects on the local network of relationships among parishioners. The term 'network' is used in the sense in which it is employed by J. A. Barnes, i.e., those contacts and relations amongst any population which are not part of the constitution of enduring groups or characteristic of definite categories of persons.[1]

The exchange of services within the parish has been greatly reduced. The bootmaker and the miller have gone: boots are bought now in town shops. The tailor has now no journeymen; after having practically gone out of business he was revived by clothes rationing during the war, for then his services came into demand for mending, and he continues on this basis. A joiner and assistant continue to enjoy a steady trade though not in joinery. They have to be prepared to do any job: wall-papering, chimney cleaning, painting, minor car and radio repairs and so forth. The joiner also has a contract with the County Education Department to run a taxi service taking children to school who live more than half a mile from it.

The blacksmith has survived too, precisely because he has taken advantage of the widening of communications which has destroyed other tradesmen and blacksmiths in neighbouring parishes. There is no longer enough work in the parish to keep him going, even though he makes some small implements for the forestry, so by a fertile stroke of imagination he and his assistant equipped themselves with a mobile smiddy, carried in an old army truck. In this the assistant visits farms over a wide area shoeing horses. That only this device has saved him from extinction is seen in the fact that the smiddys in the neighbouring parishes have all closed down. The horseshoes are bought ready-made, the smith merely fitting them on.

I have no reliable data on the amount of money spent on the

[1] J. A. Barnes, *Class and Committees in a Norwegian Island Parish*, Human Relations, Vol. VII, No. 1, 1954. See also, W. Watson and M. Susser, *Sociology in Medicine*, O.U.P. forthcoming.

goods tradesmen bring into the parish and cannot strictly
document the increasing dependence of parishioners on them,
but the fact that so many tradesmen find it profitable to come to
the parish in itself shows how much parishioners have become
dependent on them. Parishioners themselves are aware of this
and often remark on it. The dependency of Westrigg itself has
been greatly increased since 1939 by the arrival in the parish of
forestry workers. Most of the farming population raise a pig
every year and keep hens, and some keep a cow. Hence they are
independent of town supplies of bacon, eggs and milk. Few of
the forestry workers however keep animals or chickens, and all
have milk delivered daily from Broadfield, twelve miles away.
In addition to buying from visiting tradesmen parishioners shop
regularly in Craigton and in the largest town in the county on
Saturdays. The elderly, contrasting the present with the past in
this respect, remark sardonically that during the winter of
1947 when Westrigg was cut off from the towns for a week by
snowdrifts – 'Some of the younger ones just about panicked.
They thought they would starve to death.' In their youth being
cut off from town was no cause for panic; it was the normal
state of affairs.

This increased dependency can also be indirectly documented
from changes in the types of food consumed. Porridge twice a
day made from local meal is now a thing of the past (the mill
itself is now in ruins); cereals have replaced it on the breakfast
table. Sheep which die on the hill are rarely eaten. A supply of
meal is no longer part of the bargain between farmer and servant. Shop-bought bread is eaten as much as home-baked scones,
and processed foods like semolina and creamola are as popular
here as elsewhere. A great deal of locally grown vegetables are
eaten, yet fresh fruit and vegetables are sold by the tradesmen all
the year round.

These changes are not peculiar to the Borders of Scotland. Rees
in his survey of the Welsh parish notes that its recent history
shows an increasing dependence on 'consumption goods produced elsewhere'. There are now (in the parish he studied) no
tailors, shoe-makers, furniture-makers or dress-makers, while
'generally speaking the function of the wheelwright and the
smith has changed from making implements to repairing the
products of factories – even horsehoes are imported ready-made'.

'Thus', he concludes, 'apart from certain items of food, Llanfi-hangel imports practically all its requirements as finished goods, and its material culture retains little that is distinctive'.[1] Similarly, Arensberg notes that even in rural Ireland where small farming economy is still largely on a subsistence basis 'nearly all of (the craftsmen) except the smith, their peer, have been swept away before the skill of the townsmen and factory'[2]. Finally, V. Bonham Carter describes these same changes as having occurred in the English Village.[3]

With the abolition of the School Board parishioners now have no control over the affairs of the school. The teacher is appointed without reference to them and is not answerable to them for his or her work; the finances of the school are managed by the Education Committee of the County Council. Nor is the teacher so independent in his work, a curriculum and time-table being laid down by the County Education Authority. The teacher never dares to close the school on his or her own initiative – holidays are strictly controlled by the same body.

Earlier it was pointed out that the parish school was the only one the children of the parish ever attended, leaving at thirteen to take up employment on some farm, and that this restricted their experience of the world outside the parish. Now with the school leaving age at 15 and parish schools permitted to give education only up to the age of 12, every child has to attend a secondary school in some town for three years, either in Broad-field or Craigton. So before leaving school the children have some notion of what town life is like and are aware of other jobs besides herding or labouring on a farm. Many parishioners blame this practice of sending the children to town for causing 'rural depopulation'.

Increase of leisure hours, of wages, and the availability of transport have made it possible for parishioners to participate in entertainments in town. Visits to the local towns on Saturday purely for entertainment are common – pubs, picture and dance halls are the most frequented places for it. A few men go to the large town fairly regularly to see football matches.

It is apparent that parishioners have become more closely

---

[1] Rees, *op. cit.*, page 27.
[2] Arensberg, *The Irish Countryman*, New York, page 62.
[3] V. Bonham Carter, *The English Village*, Penguin Books, 1951.

linked with nearby towns. This process culminated in 1946 in Westrigg becoming a dormitory suburb of Broadfield, for some parishioners at least. In that year Broadfield tweed manufacturers found themselves short of labour, so they subsidized a bus service into Westrigg (and surrounding parishes) to enable parish girls to take employment in the Broadfield mills. All the Westrigg girls who were employed as maidservants at the time promptly became mill-girls. There have not been any farm maids in the parish since.

I described how the unity of the parish was expressed in the interest parishioners took in each other's lives and in the institution of the clipping band. If the parish has lost its former integrity changes are to be expected here. This is indeed the case. To be a parishioner is no longer to be an object of interest to all other parishioners. There are few parishioners who know of the existence of all other parishioners. As it was thought that I knew everyone in the parish, often at dances and other public occasions I would be asked by a friend to identify some 'stranger' for him – the stranger usually being a fellow parishioner. The parish registrar, one of the few who knows every parishioner says she is similarly often asked to identify 'strangers'. The blacksmith who formerly in the course of his work got to know everyone remarked one day: 'You don't know half the buggers you see now, there's that many strangers wanderin' about the bloody place!'

The disappearance of the clipping band has already been mentioned along with other forms of mutual aid. The decline in the importance of the Church and many traditional Christian practices among the majority of the population of the country has so often been commented upon it needs no stressing here; Westrigg is no exception. There is only one congregation now, of the Church of Scotland, but whereas 'everyone' formerly attended, the average number at an ordinary Sunday service is now twelve. Interest is not entirely lacking in sacraments and ceremonies, for all have their babies baptized and church weddings are preferred to civil ones, but ministers remark that 'they only use us for these occasions because they have to'.

Sunday is no longer a day rigorously set apart from workaday profane life. I have myself helped a shepherd to build haystacks on a Sunday, he being unwilling to waste the opportunity the dry day afforded for the work. Work on Sunday is a very recent practice. The wife of a farmer who employs a manager to supervise his farm remarked that in June of 1950 'the manager came to me in great agitation one Sunday and asked if I minded if he led in that day (i.e., carted sheaves of corn from the field into the shed). He said he'd never done it in his life before but didn't like to miss such a fine day.' There are not many commercial entertainments available on a Sunday in this district but such as exist are often attended by the youth of the parish. For example, they often attend motor cycle race meetings at a village about thirty miles away in summer time.

Along with withdrawal of respect for the Sabbath has gone withdrawal of respect for the minister. His presence in a house no longer creates a situation of danger to be alleviated by the children being sent out. The present minister remarks that the children do not even salute him when they meet him on the roads. He does not any longer rebuke a person for not attending church (men say scornfully – 'he daren't try!'). A woman expressed the general attitude of the working class to the minister in the following anecdote:

'They say ministers are getting worried about falling attendances, but they have only themselves to blame. They try and ram it down your throat. Three years ago (an uncle) and (a cousin) turned up for communion. The minister said from the pulpit that it wasn't good enough just to turn up for communion and on no other day. So they decided they weren't coming again. And quite right, it sticks in your throat that'.

The three indices of secularization I have used, lack of interest in ritual, withdrawal of respect for the Sabbath and for the minister are neatly exemplified by a woman who told me that at one time she used to go to church sometimes, but that then 'the minister used to come and visit us. But he stayed for hours and bored me, so to shake him off I stopped going to church; now I don't go because I'm afraid the minister will start visiting me again and bore me'. She explained this to me while spring-cleaning one Sunday morning.

It is necessary to emphasize that by 'minister' is meant the office of minister and not the incumbent of the office at any particular time or place. This is shown in the fact that many people who never attend church and who think that 'a Minister' has no right to insist that they should, yet like the present minister as a man. When they say this they assess his worth on secular, purely personal grounds; for example, all the men admire him because he is a skilled amateur motor mechanic while some like him because when they meet him he 'doesn't talk religion'. The minister, in short, is regarded in a purely secular light and judged by the same criteria as other men. This process of stripping the office of its sacredness has gone so far that some call the ministry a trade and inquire sarcastically why ministers complain of low salaries when 'they do nothing for their money.'

Finally, as is to be expected in the circumstances described, to be an elder is not generally regarded as a signal honour and the present ones are not accorded any special respect.

Several monographs describing the changes in peasant communities which follow when the relationships of the local social organization and network are replaced by those of the modern industrial and economic system show this same process of secularization occurring in them.[1] At first sight it might seem that the more complete the first process the more complete is the process of secularization. In the communities described by Arensberg and Rees the purely local network and forms of organization are much more important than in Westrigg.[2] Kinship and neighbourhood provide the main bonds among the members of the communities and neither finds it necessary to say much about nation-wide associations like Trade Unions. Correspondingly in those communities the traditional religious institutions are supported without question. Yet I do not think that Westrigg shows such an advanced stage of secularization only for this reason. Westrigg differs from those other communities also in the greater importance of its class system; whereas in the other communities work-units are organized largely on the basis of kinship ties, in Westrigg they are organized on the basis of employer-employee relationships similar to those which obtain in industrial areas. This has an important bearing on secularization. Here I shall have to anticipate later pages of this chapter (pages 73-74) and the findings described in the next. Briefly, the main points relevant to the present context are as follows. Of the

[1] See e.g. R. Redfield, *The Folk Culture of Yucatan*, Chicago, 1941.
[2] C. Arensberg, *op. cit.*; A. Rees, *op. cit.*

five classes described on pages 56-58 only the middle three are now represented in the parish. Since the beginning of the century the farm (and now forestry) workers have adopted an increasingly critical attitude towards the two classes above them, most of the members of whom are their employers or overseers. The workers (who constitute the majority of the population) consider a minister of the church to belong to the topmost class in the parish. They do so because he is like the members of that class in speech, manners and culture, and because his friends are members of the class. The worker accordingly adopts the same critical attitude to the minister, and considers the church to be an institution belonging to the topmost class which in some vague way is part of the apparatus of control which employers deploy against him.

It has already been shown that attitudes of disrespect towards the ministry are commonly expressed. Attitudes of hostility towards the office however are expressed only by working class persons. Here are examples, expressed spontaneously:

A shepherd: 'Most ministers just mix with the top lot so why should we workin' folk go to their church?'

Another shepherd, reading in the *Daily Mail* that the church wished to abolish gambling on football pools shouted angrily: 'Just like the church – always interfering with a working man's pleasures! Christ all bloody mighty! – what pleasures do we have if we can't gamble now and then.'

A ploughman: 'ministers are always complaining they're not paid enough. They say they can't manage on five hundred a year. What about us?, we've got to manage on half that! They just want to keep up a position. It isn't as if they did anything for it – it's just a trade nowadays.' He went on to say that ministers now were just 'college boys' who had discovered they were not fit for a 'real job' so took to the ministry because it was 'cushy'. Many similar remarks could be quoted.

Where social classes are in opposition to each other the minister and with him the church must be identified with one or other of them. The following events related by a minister of the district show this unequivocally. About 1935 this minister became alarmed at the hostility that obtained between farmers and farm workers, and began to preach sermons to the effect that both were forgetting their duties as Christians. Farmers were trying to get as much work from the servant for as little payment as possible, while the servants were trying to give as little labour for as much money as possible. As far as I could gather from informants, these sermons had no doctrinaire political bias, yet several of the farmers took exception to them and began to accuse the minister of 'preaching Socialism'. One of the farmers stopped giving voluntary contributions to the church funds. When the minister asked him why, he said: 'You preach a few sermons telling the farm servant his master's his best friend and to do what his master tells him and I'll give you your voluntary contribution.' The minister was almost speechless with indignation as he told me this: 'I was being bribed, bribed – a minister, can you imagine it?'

From the account given of the incorporation of farmers and servants into nation-wide unions, of the extension of rights of citizenship, increases in money wages and leisure hours, and the buying of foodstuffs from outside the parish, it will be readily apparent that the structure of the farm has changed completely. As an overall characterization of the relation of the farm servant to the farm it was pointed out how subject he was to the will of the farmer, and how much his life and that of his family was enclosed within the farm. This is no longer the case. The former personal relation between master and servant has given way to a more impersonal one – they confront each other more as abstract administrative categories, employer and employee, whose relationship is regulated by the two unions and the State. The employee is now sufficiently protected against the danger of unemployment to resist the will of the employer if he wishes to do so.

Perhaps nothing symbolizes the new relationship as much as the new nomenclature used instead of 'master' and 'servant'. The term 'farm servant' survives only in bureaucratic literature while 'master' has all but disappeared. Instead the farmer refers to his employees as 'the men' and usually to himself as 'the farmer'; while the men refer to themselves as 'farm workers' and to their employer as 'the boss'.

The change is also strickingly reflected in the great decrease in meals supplied by the farmer to farm workers. No farmer to my knowledge provides food for his men on any occasion except clipping time (and at threshing if outside help is called in) which rarely lasts longer than five days on any farm, and on the smaller farms is over in two days. Moreover, a change is occurring in the organization of those meals still distributed. Formerly the farmer's wife herself organized the preparation and distribution of them; now on many farms this is left to one of the shepherds' wives to do.

The customs in connection with hiring and firing have disappeared. Hiring Fairs died out before the Second World War, and farmers now advertise in local newspapers if they wish to hire labour. Similarly, 'speaking time' has died out – men can be fired or give notice at any time.

The farm worker's family is no longer in any sense part of the farm, and his relations to farm and family have become segregated. To the farm he is related solely as an employee and to his family solely as father, and the roles are kept strictly separate. His wife and children do not help in the hay or harvest field, nor do his sons, if he is a shepherd, help at lambing or any other time. As a consequence, the worker's family do not receive meals from the farm-house.

This leads to the second point, that the worker and his family are no longer so dependent upon the farm for their food, nor are their lives so wholly enclosed within the farm. This latter is implicit in much that has been described already – the shorter working hours, more frequent contact with towns and higher cash wages, and the purchase of foods from tradesmen. In addition, there has been a trend towards commuting perquisites for money. Each worker still makes his secret bargain with his employer and as they are loth to talk about it I do not know how far this trend has been carried. It is certain however that few now receive either meal or potatoes, while one or two do not even have a supply of milk included in the bargain. Another item which has all but disappeared is the 'one fat sheep', most shepherds taking money in lieu.

The shepherd's relation to the farm has changed more than is the case with other workers. We described how he was 'a bit of a farmer himself in a small way' and somewhat distinguished from the others, through his ownership of the pack. The pack has disappeared throughout the Borders, except for one shepherd in Westrigg, (other shepherds say he 'very likely' receives a small money wage in addition to grazing his pack). It was in fact about the turn of the century that shepherds began to give up owning packs and to ask for money wages in lieu. Those still alive, who formerly had one, say they gave it up precisely because you could not calculate how much money you might make from it in any one year, or indeed whether you would make any. It seems to have been the shepherds themselves who wanted to give up the pack, not the farmers. Having a pack instead of wages formerly made the shepherd much more dependent on the farm than the other workers, and the abandoning of this system of payment is another expression of the effort to be no longer a 'land-tied slave' which led to the formation of the F.S.U. As a result of abandoning the pack, the shepherds have lost the little distinction they once had, and as they all admit, now are 'just farm workers, just like the others'.

The main features of change in the class system described on pages 56–58 are first, a reduction in the number of classes represented in the community; second, a redistribution of power among the classes; third, whereas formerly the system was accepted by everyone as part of the natural order of things, it became questioned by the working class (and still is).

After the First World War, the Garvels began selling their land in Westrigg, and now have none. Thus the topmost class in the old system are no longer represented in the parish. With the institution of Old Age Pensions, more adequate unemployment relief and the disappearance of any stigma attached to receipt of it, the very lowest class of tramps etc., also gradually disappeared. It had practically disappeared by the Second World War, and the full employment of the war and subsequent years finally disposed of it. During the period considered, there has been a decline in population in most rural areas, certainly in this one. This has meant less unemployment, and it may be supposed that this too has hastened the disappearance of the lowest class.

It has been implicit in the material presented in this history that the two farming classes have steadily lost power in the local structure. The abolition of the Parish Council has meant that they no longer control the measures of relief to indigents. When I said that 'the parish has no control over the education given its children' what in effect this meant was that the farming classes, from which the members of the school board were recruited, no longer have any control over the education given parish children. Most important of all, as has been shown, farmers do not now exercise such stringent control over their men as they once did, the relationship between the two being controlled by nation-wide bodies. This is not to say that the farming classes have no power over the labouring class, only that it has diminished. They themselves are aware of this (see page 108) and regret it.

The third change too, is implicit in some of the material already presented. It has been shown how the farm workers opposed the power of the farmers through the formation of a trade union. Partly perhaps as an extension of this opposition but also (one gathers from informants) from indignation, members of the labouring class began to object to the arrogant manner in which the farming classes treated them in daily intercourse. A middle-aged workman's wife recalls: 'When I was a girl we used to have to curtsey to the ladies, the big farmer's wives. Some of them were just . . . I won't say what, and I made up my mind if ever I had children I'd never tell them to curtsey to the likes of them.' The blacksmith, after saying how terrible it used to be always having to lift your bonnet, went on: 'It used to fair drive you off your bloody head the way they spoke to you . . . as if you weren't human. Just like they spoke to their bloody dogs. Oh, some of us used to swear I can tell you!'

To summarize: during this century the parish has been transformed by the combined effects of several processes, particularly by a re-organization of local government and extension of the rights of citizenship, a realignment of employer and employee and re-organization of their relationship, the development of public transport and an increase in the range and amount of consumer goods available for purchase. The effects on the parish have been marked. Institutions which administered to certain needs, both of the parish as a whole, and of some individual members of it, have been withdrawn from the parish, administration of these now greatly extended needs and rights is done, not by local property owners or farmers, but by professional bureaucrats distantly located. The labouring population are less dependent upon their actual local employer and correlatively the power of farmers over their men has been reduced. Increased use of money and an increase in the flow of consumer goods into the parish has reduced the exchange of goods and services among parishioners. Higher wages, more leisure time and availability of transport have enabled parishioners to participate in activities in towns.

These processes have operated inter-dependently and the effects of them have not just produced isolated changes in single institutions or relationships within the parish, but have produced general changes transforming the nature of relationships among parishioners. They have been detached to some extent from their local environment, both physical and social; there has been a dispersal of their relatedness to each other concomitant with their being drawn into a more dispersed network of contacts and relations. To adapt a phrase of Barnes' – the mesh of the social network has become larger.[1] Relationships among the population of the parish are much more like those among the population of any industrial area than they were fifty years ago. It is implicit in this that 'social class' has increasingly become relatively more important than the formation 'community'. The following chapters are devoted to an examination of the former.

It seems from various studies that as a population becomes more industrial in character, voluntary associations among it increase.[2] This has been the case in the parish in recent times. Present clubs and associations are: the mens' bowling club; the women's Rural Institute; the women's Church Guild; the Brownies; a badminton club and a dramatic society. There is also a Unionist Association though it rarely meets; and sometimes an association will be formed for some particular occasion, a Burns Club for example to organize a supper in the poet's honour.

[1] J. A. Barnes, *op. cit.*, page 54.
[2] K. L. Little, 'The Role of Voluntary Associations in West African Urbanisation', *Amer. Anth.*, Vol. 59, Aug. 1957, pages 579–596.

CHAPTER V

SOCIAL CLASS

STRATIFICATION in any population exhibits various facets according to the contexts in which and the methods by which it is examined. The techniques used in this study are described in full in Appendix II, but a brief statement of them in the order in which they were applied may be helpful here. First, listening in conversation with and among parishioners for words implying a conventional classification of persons (in terms of the criteria discussed in the next paragraph) and noting and matching examples given of actual persons and families falling within the various classes. Second, noting friendships and cliques among parishioners and placing them within these classes; also noting association and interaction among them on public occasions such as dances. Third – a device borrowed from H. Kaufman[1] – each parishioner's name was written separately on a filing card, and I asked a number of persons to arrange the cards into social classes. The results of these classifications are shown in Table of Class Placements, Appendix II. During and after each placement I discussed the subject with the informant.

My intention was to determine those formations Weber called 'status groups', strata distinguished by the degree of social honour or prestige accorded them.[2] In any system of such groups there are restrictions on social intercourse between members of different strata outside the context of work and activities essential to the economic system, and each stratum displays a style of life its members are expected to live up to. Hence the data I required was such as indicated (a) breaks in association

[1] H. Kaufman, *Prestige Classes in a New York Rural Community*, Agricultural Experimental Station, Cornell University, Memoir 260.

[2] H. H. Gerth and C. Wright Mills, *From Max Weber*, Routledge & Kegan Paul, 1948, page 186.

among the population in contexts outside of work, correlated with (b) judgments of and evidence in behaviour of differences in prestige, and (c) differing styles of life.

There are three distinctions among related concepts used in the study of stratification which I wish to introduce here in order to clarify what this and the following two chapters are about. The distinctions are between:

(1) *Economic and Social Classes.* An economic class is a category of persons standing in the same position with respect to a market. This distinction of Weber's is so well known that further elaboration is unnecessary.[1] More important for this study is the fact that though the two sorts of classes are conceptually distinct, in actual social relations they influence each other. In Chapter VII, for example, I show how the economic class distinction of farmers and farm workers variously affects the relation of the sexes to the social class system.

(2) *Local and National Contexts of Stratification.* This distinction touches on both economic and social class.

(a) On a local level economic classes co-operate, as described for example on farms in Chapter II. The innocence of everyday co-operation is liable to deceive as to the other strand of the relation; on a national level they dispute as to the terms of the co-operation, through Trade Unions, occupational associations, political parties and pressure groups. The disputation, sometimes approaching a state of 'class conflict', cannot be studied in the context of a local group. Yet as the members of a local group are also members of the nation, the disputation has effects upon relations in the local group (see above pages 32-35 and pages 73-74 and below pages 131-132).

(b) The criteria, described above, used to determine social classes in a small locality obviously cannot be employed in the context of a population so large and widespread that the possibility of choosing to associate or not to associate with each other cannot ever be actualized for most individuals in it. It seems in fact that the concept of social class is of limited usefulness for studying large urban populations. The study of social mobility in Britain by D. V. Glass and associates used ratings of occupational prestige and a modified version of the Register General's classification of occupations.[2] Though

[1] Gerth and Mills, *op. cit.*, page 180–94.
[2] David V. Glass (ed.), *Social Mobility in Britain*, Routledge & Kegan Paul, 1954.

similar in some respects, the concepts of occupational prestige valid for the nation and social class valid for the local community are not identical; hence the social classes of this study differ in some respects (as described below) from the classification used by Glass.

(3) *Prestige and Esteem.* This distinction was first clearly drawn by K. Davis.[1] Prestige is the relative social honour accorded a position in a social system irrespective of the qualities of the individual or individuals occupying the position. Esteem on the other hand is the social honour an individual enjoys by virtue of his performance in one or several roles. There is no necessary connection between the two. Several shepherds in Westrigg are highly esteemed by both other shepherds and farmers, but their position in the class system is unaffected by this – they occupy the same position in it as other shepherds. Some farmers on the other hand are generally held to be inefficient, but remain in the same social class as other farmers. Parishioners were quite clear as to the distinction, pointing out for example that any farmer would listen with 'respect' to a good shepherd talking on the subject of sheep, but that in 'social life' the two would 'keep their distance'.

I turn now to the description of this system of local social class. It may clarify the exposition if I describe first the composition and some of the main social characteristics of these classes. For reasons explained below I call them an upper middle, a lower middle and a working class, composed respectively of 21, 33 and 270 persons. Occupations in the classes are.[2]

---

[1] K. Davis, 'Conceptual Analysis of Stratification', *Amer. Sociol. Rev.* 7 (1942), 309–21.

[2] In the Registrar General's scheme of social classes occupations in the parish fall into the following social classes:

Social Class	Occupation
I	Minister, probably the director of the scientific establishment.
II	All farmers, teachers, forestry managers, farm managers.
III	Foresters and Woodmen.
IV	Shepherds and other agricultural workmen.

Upper middle   Farmers, minister, director of scientific establish-
                           ment.
Lower middle   Farmers, forestry managers, schoolteacher, clerks.
Working class   Shepherds, shepherd-managers (of farms), gene-
                           ral agricultural workers, forestry labourers, post-
                           man, craftsmen.

Class and land ownership

Of a total acreage of 42,804 in the parish, 22,972 are owned by
members of the upper middle class (resident in the parish);
2,291 by resident members of the lower middle class, and about
12 by the working class. The rest is owned about half by the
Forestry Commission and half by absentee farmer-owners.

The range of size of farms in the two middle classes is:-

Upper   6,600; 6,204; 5,386; 2,176; 1,104; 1,000; 710
Lower   1,877   600; 454

Class and Property

Rateable values of property owned within the parish by class
are:

Upper middle £4,112
Lower middle   £769
Working class   £79

Ranges in rateable values of property owned by individuals
in the classes are:

Upper middle From £1,263 to nil.
Lower middle From £465 to nil.
Working   From £18 to nil.

These figures show (i) large differences in the distribution of
land and property among the classes, with a concentration of
them in the upper middle class; (ii) that a person's membership
of a class does not depend, at least in some cases, upon the
amount of land or property he owns. The question this raises, as
to what are the criteria of class status is discussed on pages 90 to
96. Meanwhile, having briefly described some of the outstanding

characteristics of the classes and the sort of occupations found in them, I turn now to parishioners assessments of themselves.

From the findings of the study by Glass and associates it appears that many townspeople imagine that farmers all belong to the same social class.[1] This is certainly not the case among the population studied here. In everyday conversation parishioners categorize each other into three classes by using the terms 'gentleman farmer', 'working farmer' and 'working folk'. There are differences in the frequencies with which persons of these categories employ the terms; those designated 'working farmers' and 'working folk' use all three terms much oftener than those designated 'gentleman farmer'. The 'gentlemen farmers' rarely use the term to refer to themselves, and do not often speak of 'working farmers' either, preferring the term 'small farmer'.

There are many other synonyms the classes apply to each other, e.g. 'cottagers', used by gentlemen and working farmers for 'working folk', when the conversation proceeds on the assumption that the classes exist comfortably together, as opposed to 'these people', when the talk is about labour difficulties. When working folk want to sneer at the 'gentlemen farmers' they call them 'the aristocracy of Westrigg'. Working farmers, with more irony than sneer, sometimes refer to them as 'that crowd'. Another set of terms used is 'top lot', 'middle lot' and 'bottom lot'. They may be used as a set or along with other names; they are more frequently used by forestry personnel than by those in agricultural occupations.

The local terms, gentlemen and working farmers, and working folk, obviously imply a classification of the agricultural population and of forestry labourers. Moreover, there is concensus among all parishioners concerning which persons the terms apply to. There is even a 'theory of class' heard most frequently among working folk to the effect that gentlemen farmers are people who do not need to work to make their farms pay while the working farmer, because he owns a smaller farm, has to give his own labour to it, and working folk are those who do not own farms or other substantial property and who labour or work with their hands for a living. This theory is probably true as regards the working farmer, for at any rate they all do work in varying degrees, but it is not accurate as regards gentlemen

[1] D. V. Glass (ed.), *op. cit.*

farmers, most of whom work in the sense of supervising an estate, some of whom choose to labour on their farms from time to time, and one or two of whom have to labour to make their farms yield the income they want. One of them is even called, by the working folk, 'the hardest working man in Westrigg'. Moreover the professional people in the parish are distributed between the two 'farming classes'. Informants placed them in those classes for various reasons (see pages 90-96) but mainly because their friends (within the parish) were in those classes, and because they did not labour and were obviously richer than working folk. Mainly for this reason I do not follow the local terminology in naming the classes.

Another reason is that all parishioners declare that outside the parish other classes exist which are not represented in the parish. Above the gentlemen farmers are 'the county' (see page 56). Many parishioners can remember when the Duke of Garvel 'strode like a lion through the place', and several farm workers have been employed on estates belonging to members of the county. Most of the men among the working folk declare that the 'real gentlemen' are only to be found in the county class, and some regret there are none in the parish 'to keep that crowd (gentlemen farmers) in order'. Parishioners also mention a class found in towns which they place below 'working folk' and call 'the slum class'. They had experience of the town slum class during the war when they had some of them billeted in their farms and cottages. Particularly shocking to all parishioners was the discovery that mothers of this class could not knit, sew, cook or in general care for children properly. Though parishioners associate 'slum class' with towns, from time to time a family may arrive in the parish whom the working folk quickly label with the term (see pages 123-4). As one of the habits of such families is to fall into debt with local tradesmen then move elsewhere, they do not stay long in Westrigg or the numerous parishes in the district like it. I have been reliably informed that such families are found in considerable numbers in one district on the English border where farmers employ them at rates of pay considerably lower than the minimum fixed by the wages board.

That the classes are viewed as superior and inferior to each other is soon apparent in conversation. When identifying a third party for me informants would say, e.g., 'he's not a working farmer, he's *only* a working man' or 'he's not a gentleman farmer, just a working farmer.' An upper-middle class man once remarked of agricultural labourers 'of course some of these people are hardly better than animals in intelligence and way of living.' Sometimes irritation at one provokes sweeping condemnation of the class as when a farmer exclaimed *à propos* some minor lapse on the part of a shepherd, 'they're all alike these people, they just can't think.' A lower middle class woman remarked of a working class neighbour, 'you can see the lower element coming out even in her.' A view of the working class widely held among both the middle classes is that they are 'childish'. Direct remarks like these are not very common: more common is the indirect and quite unmalicious reference like this by a farmer, 'This morning a stranger passed by the field where I was working and said "good morning" to me as if I were just a labourer. I was quite pleased, in fact a lifelong ambition of mine has been to be treated as if I were nobody.'

The attitude of the upper-middle class to the lower middle is one more of condescension, as if the latter were only poor imitations of themselves; they speak of them as 'nice people', 'steady fellow', or 'hard worker'. They do not use these phrases of each other. Occasionally one may hear a remark which reveals more openly the attitude of the upper middle to the lower middle, as when an upper-middle class mother complained that the trouble with Westrigg was that there were no children of the right age her own could play with (when at home during the school holidays). I pointed out a lower-middle class family with children of the same age, 'Oh them!' she said in disgust.

While the working class can sneer at the others on its own occasions, individuals often indicate in remarks that they generally accept the hierarchy of value which the class system represents. A ploughman discussing the embarrassment that arises when the classes attempt to mix socially said, 'Supposing that X (upper middle) comes into the Public Hall, you can tell that he's in fair misery and wants to go. He couldn't talk to me and I couldn't talk to him. He'd bore me and I'd bore him. His standards are too high.' A craftsman, 'Working folk often put a brick wall round themselves. Some of the older top lot, they won't mix with you socially but they might stop and chat with you in the street; now some working men will pass them by, they won't stop and chat. That's because some of them are ashamed of being working folk; others feel they would be deserting their own class.' Explaining why working class clubs sometimes have difficulty in getting leaders one said, 'If you get fifty working folk in a club or anything and one is chairman they won't agree. But get one (a chairman) from a higher social class and they will.' Asked why this was he said, 'It's envy; they won't recognize that the working man has any more gifts than they have. But if the chairman is say, a farmer, then they can't say that about him.'

The attitude of the classes to each other is more clearly revealed in a certain form of behaviour which is constantly occurring and in comments on it. 'They think themselves above us' is the normal comment of one class on the next above it. One lower-middle class woman said that upper-middle class women 'make me sick the way they go about thinking themselves so superior to you.' I asked how she knew they thought so and she explained, 'Well, if you're speaking to one of them you can't tell because she might be quite friendly and speak to you without any airs. But if another of their kind comes on the scene, then the one who was talking to you begins to talk to the other and soon they're edging away from you and before you know where you are you're left alone.' Working class people can also give numerous instances of this rejection of themselves in casual interaction by members of both the middle classes (and I observed many); a ploughman commented, 'it just shows you they think we're not good enough to talk to.'[1]

[1] The opposite of this kind of rejection ought to occur sometimes too, i.e., two persons of a lower class reject one of a higher. I have never observed such an interaction nor did anyone comment on it. There are several possibilities here: (a) it never does happen; (b) the person of higher status moves off before the other two have had time to reject him, thus forstalling them; (c) the person of higher status simply interprets such an interaction as an instance of the lack of manners which he is already convinced is an attribute of people of lower status and pays no more attention to it; (d) – but one can go on almost indefinitely sketching in possible norms of interaction, all equally possible, none demonstrably final. Status, as well as being a position in a social system, is also a cocoon muffling the higher in contacts with the lower, so that he does not have to pay any attention to the content of such contact if he does not want to. This of course is one of the sources of the resentment of the lower.

The preference for the company of a member of one's own class is quite separate from friendships. In some of the examples of rejection of a person of a lower class which I witnessed the class peers were not friends.

So far I have considered situations in which persons of a higher class reveal by their behaviour that they consider members of their own class more worthy of attention than members of a lower. There are situations in which members of a lower class show that they also consider members of a higher class more worthy of attention than their own. This is rarely shown in informal behaviour as described above, for a person of a lower class who constantly seeks the company of a higher is stigmatized as a social climber by his or her own class and is apt to be unpopular. This in itself illustrates the present theme, for while there are a few social climbers in each class, no one is accused of seeking the company of a lower class.

A consideration of office bearers in clubs or associations in which the majority of members are working class shows that deference is paid the higher by the lower class. Persons of higher class occupy offices much more frequently than persons of lower. The W.R.I., for example, was instituted in 1922. Until 1930 office bearers were:

President	Upper middle
Vice-President	Upper middle
Secretary	Lower middle
Treasurer	Lower middle

There were few changes in this composition until 1940. Since then working class women have began to hold office though the two key positions, President and Secretary, have always been held by the middle classes. A working class member was elected once but resigned after a few meetings, claiming that she was not educated and that it wasn't 'her place' to run the branch. What happens when a working class member cannot recognize where her place is has for some years been illustrated by a breakaway branch of the Institute formed by several members dissatisfied with the main one. The members are, like the main one, mostly working class. Every year they elect the same working class woman as president; she invariably refuses office. (She is very popular with the other women; this refusal being sometimes instanced in her favour.) They then elect another working class woman, a relative newcomer to the parish, who accepts. The rest openly jeer at her efforts to control the affairs and meetings of the branch, and sneer at her as being 'above herself'. Meanwhile a middle class woman has since its inception been elected annually to the secretaryship of the branch, has the confidence of members, and is accepted as the person who 'really runs it'.[1]

The elected committee of twelve which administers the affairs of the public hall shows the same concentration of office in the middle classes, there being usually six or seven to six or five working class members. At its meetings the working class defers to the middle class, e.g., after a meeting concerning the rebuilding of the hall a lower middle class committee member met one of the working class committee members and, 'he said the architect's fee was too high; they ought to have got a practical builder for the job; it would have saved a lot of money. I said "now you were at the meeting when that was discussed. X (upper middle) stood up and said he was not going to have anything to do with it unless a qualified architect was going to do it, and Y (upper middle) seconded the proposal. That was the time to object . . . but nobody did and you were there." "Oh," said he, "but nobody says anything against them".' It is perhaps superfluous to add that though the majority of committee members, i.e., working and middle class members were in private against the proposal to employ an architect rather than a builder, the upper-middle class minority had their way.

Among male parishioners deference is institutionalized in the naming system, the essence of which is that a person of higher class status may address a person of lower class by his Christian name but the person of lower status must address the person of

---

[1] In a recent publication, *Village on the Border*, Cohen & West, 1957, R. Frankenberg analyses the social tensions which prevent the voluntary associations in a Welsh village from flourishing. There, persons of higher status are often asked to take office in the local associations in order that no one in the village can be held responsible for the failure of the association. Frankenberg's analysis seems to me admirable. The situation in the Welsh village, however, seems to be very different from that in Westrigg, where the associations continue despite occasional quarrels and where the person of higher status is still very much part of the whole community despite his participation in society outside (see Chapter VII).

higher status by the title of 'Mr.' followed by the surname. 'Mr.' is a symbol of middle class status; the men of the working class always address each other by Christian names and are apt to think they are being made fun of if addressed by 'Mr.' One whom I addressed in this way said: 'Don't call me Mister. I haven't reached that status and probably never will.' Middle class men address each other as 'Mr.' if they are not close friends. They expect this deference from the working class, as the latter know. As one said, 'X (upper middle) can come up to me and say "Hello Jimmy" as if we were great friends, in fact he does, but he'd be damned annoyed if I said to him "Hello John".'

The foregoing paragraphs have already illustrated 'restrictions on social intercourse' between members of different classes in informal contacts and chance encounters. Some qualification is necessary to avoid giving the impression that all such contacts merely illustrate the rejection of a lower class person by a higher for there is often some sort of friendly if brief contact between persons of different class. For example, on market days in town a farmer sometimes has a drink with his own men. Or sometimes a middle class woman will drop in on a working class woman for a cup of tea. However, though such meetings are amicable, the interaction is almost invariably different in form or tone from interaction between members of the same class. With regard to form, the interaction is non-reciprocal; the farmer is standing his men a drink as an acknowledgement of good work done and the arrangement is quite different from the normal reciprocity of drinking among friends. Sometimes, instead of drinking with them a farmer simply gives his men the money to buy a drink. Similarly the middle class woman who drops in does not invite the working class women to her own house for tea, nor does the latter ever try dropping in on the former. Occasionally a middle class man in a genial mood will try drinking with working class men. Usually one of two modes of interaction result. Either his geniality is accepted at its face value and he is replied to in the same tone, in which case after a short exchange of banalities the interaction is broken off. Or else his geniality contains a note of challenge, as if he were daring the others to reject him outright. Occasionally (I was told) this happens, but mostly the working men respond with a note of humourous threat. This interaction is liable to last a long time, with the parties hinting more and more openly at each other's shortcomings.

Restrictions on association in more enduring bonds between members of different classes is even more clearly visible: cliques and (with a few exceptions discussed later) friendships are formed within a class and do not include members of different classes.[1] On market days and Saturday night in town, groups of friends can be seen together, and in the parish one soon learns the cliques who meet in each others houses. These relationships are so apparent that on checking my list of them with two parishioners our observations tallied almost exactly. There seem to be differences in class systems in the degree to which friendship across class boundaries is possible. From a comparison of various studies it seems that cross-class friendship is normal in urban areas but not in rural.[2] This is probably because of their very visibility in rural society. It is possible to segment one's relationships in urban society, one can have friends who are not friends of each other, who do not know of each other's existence. Such segmentation is impossible in rural society, where any single friend knows whom else one associates with and loyalties have to be affirmed in a more unequivocal way than in urban society.

The issuing of formal invitations to private hospitality is a custom of the upper-middle class; dinner and cocktail parties are attended by members of it. Another institution of the same sort found only among this class (in the parish) is the shooting party. Local dances on the other hand are mainly a working class institution – promoted, organized and mainly attended by them, though a few lower-middle class persons may sometimes attend them.

Even when the classes are present under one roof the gap in association is still clear. 'You should have been here during the war', said one informant,'then you'd have seen the social classes all right. If there was a dance or whist drive or anything to raise comforts for the troops the whole parish used to come. But you'd see them in the hall in three separate groups. They only mixed with their own kind.' Where the middle classes were represented

[1] See Appendix 2.

[2] Compare e.g., J. West, *Plainsville, U.S.A.*, New York, 1945, with W. L. Warner and P. S. Lunt, *The Social Life of a Modern Community*, Yale, 1941.

at W.R.I. Christmas parties etc., the various social categories arranged themselves in the hall as in this diagram.

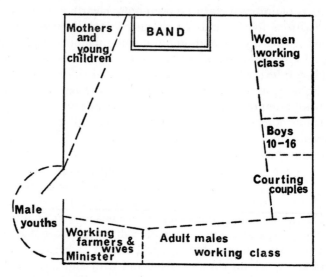

Pattern of association at a dance.

The only times when the boundaries of this formation were crossed were when occasionally a middle class mother would join the others at the fireplace. The phrase 'they only mix with their own kind' was the commonest one working class informants used to describe the nature of the local social classes. An upper-middle class man commented à propos of this characterization, 'Well if I mixed with everybody, association with me wouldn't be of much value to anybody, would it?'

Of all the forms of social intimacy courtship and marriage express social equality more than any other. This, along with other specially indicative forms of association such as commensality, is treated in full in Chapter VII (pages 117–122). Here it is only necessary to say that in the vast majority of extant marriages among parishioners both partners are of the same social class.

In several studies of social classes in industrial society it has been found that each class tends to favour particular types of voluntary association and leisure time activity.[1] Tendencies of this sort are apparent in the class system of the parish, for example only working class men regularly attend the carpet bowling club, while only upper-middle class people regularly attend meetings of a bridge club in a nearby town. However, differentiated participation in voluntary associations within the parish is determined as much by sex difference as by class differences, hence is treated in the section on sex and class (pages 122-137).

The patterns of association examined here, when correlated with the expressions of attitudes of superiority and inferiority cited in previous pages, indicate unequivocally the presence of social classes in the community. Intimate association functions as an indicator of social equality and as diagnostic of the class status of individuals, not only for the inquiring observer, but also for the parishioner. For example, the scientific establishment employs several assistants with various specialist qualifications. They do not normally stay long in the place, and rarely associate with any parishioners. For this reason informants refused to place them in any social class (see Table of Class Placements, Appendix II), making comments like 'they don't mix with anybody – just themselves,' or 'they're a community all to themselves.' Or again, some working class informants hesistated before allotting the minister to a social class on the grounds that 'he has to associate with everybody'. On thinking about it, however, they distinguished his duty visits in the role of minister from his associations by choice off duty, and placed him by the latter.

However, though restrictions on social intercourse are of the utmost diagnostic value, it must be admitted that there are exceptional instances – that a few people associate intimately across 'class boundaries'. The exceptions are few, but that there are some raises the question as to whether or not there are class boundaries, or in what sense there are. Before dealing with this question I shall finish describing the local class system by considering the determinants of class status.

The attitudes of the classes to each other and restrictions on

---

[1] W. L. Warner and P. S. Lunt, *op. cit.*; A. B. Hollingshead and F. C. Redlich, *Social Class and Mental Illness*, Wiley, 1958. H. M. Johnstone, *Sociology*, Routledge & Kegan Paul, 1961. B. Barber, *Stratification*, New York, 1957.

association between them do not explain how a person comes to be allotted to one rather than another. To answer the question, what are the criteria by which class status is evaluated, is to explain why one class has more prestige than another. In the initial description of the classes I showed that within a higher class more land and property is found than in a lower. It is not, of course, the classes who own the property, but individuals and since (as shown on page 79) there are individuals in the two middle classes who do not own any, it is clear that this criterion by itself does not explain how prestige is awarded. From both the concentration of property in the two middle classes and remarks of informants such as those quoted below however, it is also clear that it is one very important criterion. Others specially mentioned by informants were power or authority, education, and several customs, standards and usages – such as good manners, speech and accent – which can be considered as components of a style of life.

Authority or power was explicitly singled out by only men, and invariably meant authority and power in the context of employer-employee relations. Working class men tended to stress power while middle class men tended to stress authority. Employers of labour obviously wield power in the sense of being in the position to hire and fire, and in addition a farmer's power of influencing a workman's chances of employment in a district are by no means negligible. Farmers in any one district are in an informal compact as over against workman, shown in this farmer's description of hiring. 'You advertise in the papers and wait and hope someone will answer. Then when you get an answer you ring up his employer and ask "are you finished with this man" – "yes" – "is he any good?" –"wouldn't touch him with a barge pole" – "all right, thank you". Eventually you meet a man and tell him the conditions he'll work under. . . .' When a workman leaves a job he is given a written testimonial containing no adverse judgments, which he knows to be worthless. A shepherd said, 'You only ask for the testimonial because if you didn't get one your neighbours would think there was something far wrong. But the bosses talk about you on the telephone to each other. That's where they have you.' Several workmen cited cases of alleged victimization, in which a farmer prevented an employee he had sacked from finding another job.

By authority, men of all three classes meant the authority exercised by an employer in the day to day supervision of his labour team. The following tables indicate the amount of power and authority found in each class.

If the two forestry managers are excluded since they hire and fire on behalf of the forestry commission (and also the director of the scientific establishment for similar reasons), the amount of labour employed by each class is:

Class of Employer	No. of Employers	No. of Employees	Class of Employees	Ratio of Employer/Employee
Upper Middle	7	43	Working class	1/6
Lower Middle	4	8	Working class	1/2
Working class	2	2	Working class	1/1
Including forestry managers the figures for Lower Middle are:				
Lower Middle	6	39	Working class	1/6.5

However, if we consider the range of power of this sort wielded by individuals within each class, it is apparent that the amount of power an individual has does not determine his class status. Ranges are:

(a) Excluding Forestry Managers

Class of Employer	Highest No. of Employees per Individual	Lowest No. of Employees per Individual
Upper Middle	14	0
Lower Middle	6	0
Working	1	0

(b) Including Forestry Managers

Class of Employer	Highest No. of Employees per Individual	Lowest No. of Employees per Individual
Upper Middle	14	0
Lower Middle	17	0
Working	1	0

Education as a criterion was mentioned by both sexes of all classes.

At present children of the upper-middle class get their schooling in boarding schools outside the parish. Lower-middle class children attend the parish and local schools until 15, when they may be sent to boarding schools. Working class children attend the parish and local schools.

Amount of formal education varies, university degrees of honours standard being common in the upper middle class, rare in the lower middle class, and totally absent in the working class. Though it is likely that a member of a higher class will have received more formal education than a member of a lower, this in itself does not determine class status. A few men in both middle classes do not have the school leaving certificate, as is the case with all but two men in the working class.

Examination of occupations associated with the classes shows again that type of occupation is closely correlated with class position but that in one important instance, farming, persons in the same occupation can be in different classes. However, it was clear from informants remarks while making class placements that some occupations carry a fateful prestige, in the sense that all individuals in the category are bound to occupy the same class status. This was most evident in the case of farm and forestry workers. Regularly when an informant was asked for a list of names of persons belonging to the working class he would start by naming . . . x, y, z, etc., but would soon cease naming persons and turn to occupations, ending with '. . . forestry labourers, shepherds and people like that'. At the other end of the (local) social scale was the case of minister. Of this calling, upper-middle class people would deplore its emoluments, so low that 'the minister can't live like a gentleman any more', but nevertheless included him in their class because 'the minister always is'. That some of the working class occupations are unequivocal in status was also apparent from the way informants handled the cards while sorting them. Persons in these unequivocal positions were immediately disposed of, while there was hesitation over the others.

It is clear that none of these factors by itself determines class status, and that none by itself provides the scale of value by reference to which the prestige of the classes can be measured.

Instead there seems to be in the community an implicit notion of a 'class quota'. It is as if points were awarded on the basis of all the values considered and a total allocated. This was clear from the way informants made their class placements. For example X (upper middle) commented on Y, 'I know his farm's small . . . but he's the same background as myself, Rugby and Selwyn', and placed him in the upper-middle class. Or working class informants placing a craftsman often made remarks like this. 'He's quite rich, but after all he's only a craftsman, just a working man.' Or a farmer placing a titled gentleman farmer, 'His farm's no bigger than mine, he can't make all that much from it . . . but he's got that title – you can't get past that!'

Some such notion as 'class quota' seems required to account for the ease and speed with which 'strangers' who settle in the parish are placed in one or other of the three classes. For example, some of the gentlemen farmers in Westrigg and surrounding parishes are recent immigrants to the district, having come to farming after distinguished careers in business, the professions or some branch of the civil service. Many of them (in the district) have taken over 'small farms', i.e., farms as small as those owned or leased by lower-middle class farmers. Yet these strangers were immediately recognized as upper-middle class or 'gentlemen farmers' by their class peers and the other classes on the basis of their past careers and the education and wealth these careers implied. Other strangers, e.g. forestry employees, are just as speedily placed.

Against the suggestion that parishioners, in allocating class status, judge people in terms of a quota of prestige appropriate to each class, it may be said that behind all the factors considered lies wealth conceived of as purchasing power, and that an examination of the distribution of wealth among parishioners would show the base values for status judgements. There is one good reason why wealth has not been considered as a separate factor here, and that is that neither I nor informants know how much of it each parishioner has and it is considered the height of bad manners to inquire. As a farmer said, 'It can't be money that makes class for nobody here knows how much another man has. We keep that secret.' This attitude is general among parishioners. For example, it is extremely rude to approach a van while someone else is making a purchase from it. This, it was explained, is because it is rude to discover how much another is spending. Against this it can be said that everyone knows roughly the scale of workmen's wages and of the professional people, and moreover that wealth becomes visible in what a person actually buys. What is bought goes to make up a 'standard of living', items of which function as symbols of class status (see next chapter).

There are two questions involved here: one concerns the element of time and mobility in the class system; the other, critical points at which one or other factor becomes decisive in the allocation of status. As to the first, it is obvious from material already presented that, at any given moment, relative amount of wealth is not the sole determinant of status; most parishioners thought that some of the craftsmen were as rich as some of the lower-middle class people, and richer than one or two of the upper-middle class (e.g., the minister). It is equally obvious that increase of wealth enables a family or individual to purchase symbols of the class above, and that loss of wealth forces a family to accept the symbols of a lower class. Mobility in general is treated in the next chapter. From the few cases of recent relative increases and decrease of wealth which the community affords, the only generalization it is possible to make is that changes in relative wealth do not affect a family's status during the lifetime of the head of it – *within the community*. Within the community, that is, the time span of the class quota is longer than a generation. As to how much longer, and as to whether this situation ever constitutes a motive for movement out of the local community, I have not the material to judge.

The second question seems to me greatly neglected in discussions of social class, for the sociological problem of determining how class status is allocated cannot be solved solely by pointing to so many factors, all of which are already known, or by an arbitrary decision that one or other is 'fundamental'. What is important it that at different points in the system different factors become of crucial importance in the allocation of status. This again was clear from comments of informants while making class placements. An area where there was much hesitation in judgment (among informants of all classes) was the distinction between craftsmen and the smaller working farmers. A craftsman may own no more property than a bag of tools and a motor car, yet his income can be as sizeable as a small farmer's. A craftsman may be in a position of authority over an apprentice or may hire a young assistant, and though in such a relationship the teacher/pupil note will often sound, the craftsman has ultimate sanctions at his disposal not greatly different from those a small farmer has *vis-à-vis* an employee. In this area too it is often difficult to make a distinction between craftsman and farmer on the basis of 'standard of living' or style of life. Yet all informants eventually did draw a distinction solely on the basis of the sheer fact of land ownership (it being understood that 'land' meant a holding large enough to be an independent business enterprise). 'After all', they would say, 'he does own a farm, and (X the craftsman) doesn't.'

Higher up the system neither the sheer fact of property ownership nor its amount distinguishes between one class and another, the professional people having none and several upper-middle class farmers having holdings as small as those of lower-middle class farmers. The point in land-values where factors other than size of farm come into play (in this community) seems to be at about 2,000 acres. Above this size farmers are all of the upper-middle class, and sheer size is an important qualification; of one farmer a class peer remarked 'he gets in (to our class) of course just because his farm's so big.' Below this size the farmer may be of either class. The other factors brought to bear on status judgments at this point with regard to both farmers and professionals are education and 'background', style of life and estimate of relative income. Though I call these 'factors' as if they were four clearly distinguishable variables, informants did not in fact separately specify them as such. None used the actual term 'style of life', though women informants obviously meant this when they stressed the importance of good manners, eating customs and size of house as determinants of status. It is difficult to see how anyone could sharply separate these variables without doing a great deal of research on the matter, which of course informants are much too busy to do. Style of life is obviously connected with income and expenditure, and it was clear from interviews that education was a feature of background; which latter included also previous occupation and personal history. I had the impression that when they mentioned these variables informants were all indicating the same thing, and rather than

95

attempt to separate them and measure their relative importance as status determinants I shall describe in the next chapter the class cultures in which they became visible. The distinction implicit in these considerations between the lived-in order (for informants) and the analysed order (for the anthropologist) I discuss below.

It is implicit in the data presented above that the class system of the parish cannot be represented as three distinct groups sharply demarcated one from another so that boundaries are clearly apparent between adjoining classes. There is obviously a certain indefiniteness about it – a feature of class systems in industrial society which has often been commented upon (see refs. page 89). The area of indefiniteness in the system calls for some explanation but first it must be described. Briefly, the position is that while the upper-middle class is sharply distinguished from the lower-middle class there is not the same clarity of boundary between the latter and the working class. Taking the criterion of association this means that while members of the upper-middle class do not associate with members of the other two classes, some members of the lower middle sometimes associate with some members of the working class.

As described on page 94 informants hesitated before making a status distinction between some of the lower-middle class farmers and some of the craftsmen, and it is particularly in this area that the boundary between the two classes is blurred. A small farmer may have one or two friends who are craftsmen or shepherd-managers, the friends visiting each other to play draughts, cards or just to talk. An elderly lower-middle class widow, long resident in the parish, has a few friends among the long resident working class women. There are several points to note about these few stable associations: first, the lower-middle class people concerned have usually some prior connection with the working class, such as having been borne into it and having moved into the lower middle in their own lifetime, or having had a typically working class occupation for some years in youth. Second, these friendships are not the only ones the parties concerned have; the lower-middle class person always has other friends of his or her own class who do not associate with his or her working class friends, and the same principle applies to the working class people in these cross-class friendships.

In addition to regular visiting among such friends, occasionally a lower middle and a working class man will associate with each other for some one particular purpose, usually in some leisure time activity such as fishing or playing draughts. It is noticeable that in this type of inter-class association the two men never stand in the employer-employee relationship to each other in workaday life.

There are no analogous associations between the upper middle and the other two classes, no friendships or reciprocal visiting; at the most, only business contacts more or less disguised. As one lower-middle class woman said, 'Occasionally Mrs X (upper middle) asks me in to tea, but it is only to discuss the Guild or some other business: I know she's only using me', adding in reply to my question that she knew it was no use asking Mrs X to her own home as she would refuse. Another lower-middle class woman described with bitterness how in the same relationship of disguised business contact she had twice invited an upper-middle class couple to her house, only to realize eventually that they did not mean the polite acceptance with which they agreed to 'drop in some day'.

Kinship connection within the parish also illustrates this point. The ratio of connected to unconnected households in the working class is 1 : 2.2; in the lower-middle class 1 : 4.5; and in the upper middle there is no effective connection – two households are connected by a tie of second cousinship which is however ignored by the households concerned. If this connection is counted, the ratio in the upper-middle class is 1 : 4.5. The important feature of these connections for the argument here is their direction. The two upper middle households are connected with each other; none of the lower middle households are connected with each other or with the class above, all their connections being with four working class households. Apart from these four, all the connected working class households are connected with each other. The direction of the connections seems consistent with the characterization of the structure of the class system described above.

This structure, a sharp distinction between upper and lower middle and a much less clear one between the latter and the working class, is also apparent in the Table of Class Placements. Only the upper-middle class is fully agreed as to who exactly is a member of it and who is not. Amongst informants of the other two classes there is no agreement as to where the boundary between them lies. As the next two chapters show, this structure appears no matter from what aspect the system is considered. There are two main reasons for the area of indefiniteness described above. The first is a feature of all three classes, viz., within a class there are a few different ranks. Parishioners note these through asymmetry of relationship between members of the same class. As several pointed out, in the upper-middle class, when X issues an invitation to dinner, those invited invariably attend whether they like X or not, whereas X does not always respond to the invitations of the others. This, they say, means that X is 'a little above the others'. Or at public gatherings, Mrs Y is always more anxious to speak to Mrs Z than Z is to Y. This doesn't mean that each family in a class has a distinct rank; only that a few stand out as higher than the majority and a few as lower. Those recognized by their class peers as slightly higher are also singled out for special mention by people of the next higher class. Special attention is accorded them because they do in fact embody some of the values which distinguish the next higher class from their own, e.g., craftsmen not being employed by somebody else are, to that extent, like the lower-middle class farmer and may sometimes be just as rich as the latter; hence they are accorded a higher rank than labourers.

This feature of the system is closely connected with another already discussed, namely that the class status of a person or a family is not necessarily determined by reference to one single value; and since the values used in allocating status are hardly commensurable on a single scale, in the area described status can be allocated or claimed on the basis of several values.

The indefiniteness described so far is limited – association among a few persons in the area between lower middle and working class – and touches on only one of the criteria of a class system, restriction on social intercourse between adjacent classes. There is another sort of indefiniteness which characterizes the system when viewed as a whole and which touches on another of the criteria, namely judgments of prestige. This sort of indefiniteness is also connected with the fact that multiple values are used in allocating status, but cannot be reduced to that simple fact. The indefiniteness is not as to the relative prestige of the classes, but as to the values by reference to which it is accorded. Persons in different positions in the system stress different values as crucial.

Most working class men stress wealth and property as the sole determinants of class status. One said, 'it's just a matter of money and property – who has and who hasn't' and proceeded to divide the population into farmers and others; then he recalled that professional people associated with farmers and began to qualify his original placements. Another divided the upper-middle class into those he thought had a lot of money and those who hadn't: he remarked that as far as he was concerned they were really one class, but he expected they distinguished among themselves who had money and who hadn't. Another, while making class placements, remarked (almost viciously) every time he came across a card bearing the name of a gentleman farmer, 'he's got pots of money.' He came to the name of a farmer new to the parish and owning a medium sized farm, and remarked that as the farm wasn't very big he would probably be 'just a working farmer'. I said, 'but he's got pots of money'; the informant at once changed his placement of the newcomer to upper-middle class.

Women of the working class tend to stress manners, house type and eating customs, not so much as the main determinants of status, but as what in doubtful cases makes all the difference between a higher and a lower one.

The upper-middle class in making class placements never explicitly mention wealth but stress education, background and independence. One placed craftsmen in the lower-middle class for this latter reason. Apart from formal education the main features of 'background' they stress are service 'to the community' (meaning the nation) and 'experience' – the knowledge of society and institutions outside the local community which is acquired by travel, education or work. Because of the emphasis on experience and service one of the upper-middle class informants at first thought of making a status distinction between forestry and agricultural workers, on the grounds that many of the former were ex-servicemen and more sophisticated in outlook than the majority of the latter.

Lower-middle class informants, while stressing wealth and size of farm as major determinants, are also aware that these are not decisive for the status of some individuals, but at the same time are puzzled as to what else is. They assert the importance of 'character'; for this reason one placed a shepherd manager in his own class because by managing a large farm efficiently and wielding authority over the other employees the shepherd displayed a strong character. The women of this class in talking of status stress manners more than anything else. As with the working class women, however, it is not that they conceive manners to be the main determinant of status, for they rank families in the same way as other informants, but that they conceive good manners as crucial in cases where, by the other criteria, status is ambiguous. One lower-middle class woman went further than this and included in her own class several working class women who had 'good character' and 'manners like us'. She herself had been born into the working class. For further details concerning the codes of women's status judgments (see pages 127-133).

A few individuals were occasionally idiosyncratic in their class placements. For example, one craftsman noted for his versatility, wit, and socialist opinions, for whom any but the working class was a falling away from human perfection, a descent into false values of greed and snobbery, thought that nevertheless two particular farmers were plain chaps without airs, 'like us', and placed them in the working class.[1] Such occasional idiosyncratic placements, however, were made within the more general framework of class common to all.

Two individuals in performing the class placement operation provided idiosyncratic views, not of the status of one or two fellow parishioners, but of the class system itself. One, a woman, proceeded to classify parishioners according to their moral worth, so that drunkards and lazy people were at the bottom and respectable ones at the top. Another, a man, classified them according to the interest they took in community affairs. Interestingly enough, both these informants were in positions within the objective 'area of indefiniteness' described above. Both, too, indicated while making these placements that they were aware of the class system I have been describing. For their placements were made in opposition to it, e.g., each remarked several times when placing some high status person low down in his (or her) moral system – 'I know everybody else thinks X is very high up

---

[1] This attitude seems to be prevalent among urban working classes. See F. Zweig, *The British Worker*, Pelican Books, 1942.

but in my opinion he's only (a drunkard, a selfish man, etc., etc.).'

This sort of indefiniteness in no way qualifies the picture of the class system as I have presented it in terms of patterns of association and of display of qualities and possessions. On the contrary, the stereotyping of evaluations in accordance with position in the system indicates that a class tends to be a complete social milieu for its members[1]. Hence a description of the system needs to be completed by an account of each class as a 'social milieu', i.e., an account of class cultures: this I do in the following chapter. A description of class cultures will also help to answer two questions which arise from the material and discussion presented above – first, what is the nature of the formation labelled 'social class system', and second, how does the anthropologist's picture of it tally with the experience of it of those from whose behaviour and words he constructs his picture?

[1] An especially good account of the perspectives through which each class views the total class system (in an American town) is given in A. Davis, B. B. Gardner and M. B. Gardner, *Deep South*, Chicago, 1941.

CHAPTER VI

CLASS CULTURES

SOCIAL classes can be thought of as cultural categories, for the various classes have some different forms of standardized behaviour and material culture. As every class is not a discrete entity there are many qualifications to be made to the idea of 'class culture'. The structure of the system analysed in the preceding chapter appears in culture also, so that while it is easy to describe upper middle and working class cultures, there are difficulties in attempting to describe a culture for the lower middle class which could be said to be characteristic. Accordingly I shall contrast upper-middle class culture with working class culture here, adding only a few notes on that of the lower-middle class. There are many other qualifications to be made, but if the idea of 'class culture' is accepted as a merely regulative one I need not list them, and they will become apparent to the reader in this and the following chapter. Since some selection has to be made among all the traits that distinguish the classes I shall describe here only those which function most conspicuously as symbols of class status – house, clothing, meals, form and content of speech.

The house is the most obvious of these. The upper-middle class dwelling is a mansion house type of structure hidden from view behind trees. Beside it is a large garden, much of which is given over to lawns, bushes and flowers. All farm houses are close by the steading, but whereas in the lower-middle class the back door of the house opens directly on to the steading so that the farmhouse is part of it, the upper-middle class farmhouse is separated from the steading by a wall or gate or in some other way: work is separate from living. With many more rooms at their disposal than the working class, different family activities are allotted to different rooms, cooking, eating, sleeping, entertainment of visitors – each takes place in a different room.

Though all classes wear the same basic type of clothing, those worn in this class are much more expensive than those worn by the others. Some of the women of this class have a habit of boasting of the expense of their clothes. As open boasting in a joyful spirit is disapproved of here they do it by expressing indignation at the rapacity of tailors (and announcing the price) or in some other indirect way.

The dialect used by this class is very different from that used by the working class. The latter is distinctively Scottish both in vocabulary and accent. The upper-middle class avoids the Scottish dialect as it avoids (locally) involvement in distinctively Scottish culture in general – folk songs, dances, etc. Sometimes they use a Scots word in conversation in order to achieve a droll or humorous effect, demonstrating thereby their distance from the dialect of the working class.[1] An interest in Scottish culture is permitted in this class only if it partakes of the nature of 'research' into something antiquated. One, for example, takes an antiquarian delight in looking up in Jamieson's dictionary words used as a matter of course by an elderly shepherd he employs; he doesn't use the words in daily life afterwards.

The wider social contacts of this class, their position in society as property owners and producers, and their education is reflected in their conversation. Parochial events and characters are of secondary interest; they are fond of discussing political affairs both on a national and international level. They are quick to show in conversation that they know how to take advantage of public institutions – the County Council, the Department of Agriculture, etc.

They place a much higher value upon conversation than do the other classes and are much more skilful at it, deftly playing with words and keenly sensitive to the implications of changes in tone of voice, of pauses and hesitations in speech. They can converse easily about matters of little importance to them personally and enjoy the exercise of their skill in speech for its own sake.

---

[1] Distancing behaviour of this sort is perhaps only to be found within the local social context. It is possible that elsewhere, e.g. on visits to England, they occasionally exhibit an insistent Scottishness in behaviour.

Working class culture

Working class people live in cottages of two to four rooms, except for the shepherd managers and their families. Gardens are small and not much of them is given over to flowers and lawns, nor is the cottage ever hidden from sight by trees. Rooms, being few, cannot always be allotted one function; in the older two roomed cottages inhabited by a complete family it is common for one room to serve as kitchen, dining room, parlour and bedroom. Members of the household are in close contact with each other and it is hardly possible for one to isolate himself physically. Whereas in the upper-middle class three cooked meals a day is normal, in this class there is usually only one.

Apart from one suit or costume set aside for special occasions, people, especially men, have no great regard for clothes. When discussing advantages of living in the country working class people always gave as one that 'you don't need to bother about your clothes – you can wear anything all the time.'

The dialect of this class is a distinctively Scottish one. For example, when counting the men proceed – yin, twae, thri, fower, five, sax, seeven, echt, etc. Their culture in general is more distinctively Scottish than that of the other classes, for example, their favourite music is Scottish folk song and dance music. Many play the fiddle and some the bagpipes; the accordion is another instrument they play and again it is almost solely Scottish music they play on it. One of the most celebrated Border dance bands includes two Westrigg men. Their favourite dances are all Scottish country dances and there never has been a time when they were anything else – their preference is not a 'revival' of interest such as occurs from time to time in industrial towns. The only poetry they are interested in is that of Burns. They have a saying that an answer to every question in life will be found either in the Bible or in Burns.

The conversation of this class reflects the narrow range of their social contacts; a great deal of it is about parochial affairs, neighbours and work. Apart from this it is mainly about sport (among men) and housekeeping, children, and the Royal Family (among women). Shepherds wives often say their men can talk about nothing but sheep. One's personal life history may be recounted or referred to quite a lot. Conversation is not regarded as a pure skill from the use of which enjoyment can be got, but more as a means of conveying information, hence no matter what the content is there is apt to be a note of earnestness to it (information can be only true or false) which the upper-middle class finds boring. A term of praise often used among working people is 'sincere fellow' while among the upper-middle class a common term is 'good company'.

The working class tends to have specialists to exploit the possibilities of unseriousness in speech; they distinguish two types of person who are good at entertaining others – the 'wag' and the 'comic', terms never used among the upper-middle class. The wag is the person who is invariably cheerful and has a lot to say of a mildly humorous nature. The comic's is a more striking role, that of jester; he is funny both in speech and action at the expense of others. He is fully licensed in his role and no one, however he may be offended by the comic's sallies, ever dares to retaliate.

Unlike the upper-middle class the working class is not afraid of silence in a gathering and often admits implicitly that there is nothing to say. It is common for friends to sit silently round a fire for long stretches. One old shepherd if he couldn't find anything to say to a visitor simply went off to bed, without saying so. As with the comic's behaviour, this is unthinkable among the upper-middle class. As among them everyone is expected to be impersonally bright a silence in a gathering is an admission of failure. They have no way of dealing with it when it happens, and everyone simply feels uncomfortable. The working class has a way of dealing with such a silence. After a few minutes someone says with a sigh 'ay ay'. What is meant here is extremely complicated, something like 'Here we are, still alive but not quite sure why, we've said all we have to say that's worth saying and now await some grace that will enable us to say some more.' Whatever it means the expression keeps the gathering together round a meaning understood by all, integrates it against the threat the surrounding silence offers.

While the life of this class is very much confined within the parish and surrounding district and conversation on the whole reflects this, a few individuals in it seemed to me to have the widest horizons of all. For most people, and for all the middle classes life is enclosed within present day society whatever the range of social contacts a person has. A few elderly working class men, however, seemed liberated from society itself – money, status, convention, ambition, none of these touched them heavily. Among them serious (quite unpretentious) discussion of man's history and destiny can be heard. They are much less bound down by time than other people. For example, one told me of a plague of mice which swept Westrigg thirty years ago (an authentic event). They ate so much herbage that on some hills there was none left for the sheep. When I expressed surprise he added in a tone of slight rebuke that there was nothing surprising about a plague as they had them constantly in Biblical times. They do not think of themselves, some of these elderly shepherds, as employees getting a wage by selling a skill to an employer but hold that shepherds are in the world to look after sheep, which could not survive without shepherds. If this is questioned they say there never has been a time when there were sheep without shepherds to look after them, as the Bible shows.

Lower-middle class culture

Different families in this class combine in different ways traits of the cultures of the other two; all remain distinct from the upper-middle class while a few are hardly distinct from the working class.

A curious silence surrounds it in the parish, for while the other two classes have plenty to say about each other and distinguish 'characters' in the other round whom they gossip or tell amusing stories, neither mentions the lower-middle class much. Perhaps the most general remark that can be made about the culture of this class is that there is a certain reserve towards all cultural forms and a certain stress on character and manners. In some individuals this reserve appears as a genuine modesty, e.g., they would discuss political events with as much insight as the upper-middle class but without the authoritative note, without suggesting they knew exactly what to do; in other individuals it appears as a perhaps timid incomprehension.

In its equivocal position and containing within itself a greater diversity of behaviour patterns than either of the two other classes, the lower-middle class is the area where the meaning of all exterior cultural forms nowadays becomes most questionable.

As such, it is on a national level in films and books, often the butt of sarcastic humour; on a local level it is apt to be the subject of patronage from above, 'they're nice people', or ridicule from below, 'they're really only working folk.'

It is possible that the ideas and attitudes of each class cohere into separate ideologies. Though I did not attempt a detailed enough examination of the matter to come to any definite conclusion I doubt if this would be found to be the case. As an illustration of the complexity of the problem political attitudes may be considered. There is first the difficulty of discovering what attitudes people in fact do have. Only about a dozen working men belong to the local (parish) branch of the Unionist Association but this does not mean that the rest vote for a party opposed to the Conservatives. Several who do vote Conservative said they refused to join the U.A. because of the embarrassments and constraints that arise when people of different classes attempt to mix. Moreover working class people are very secretive about how they vote because, they say, if political allegiance became known quarrels might arise between friends or a labour voter be discriminated against by his boss. To complicate matters further many working class women say they never vote or think about politics because that is 'men's business'. As the M.P. for the constituency is Liberal-Unionist, opposed at the last election by a Labour candidate, it seems that the majority of working men here do not vote Labour.

That all middle class adults belong to the Unionist Association does not necessarily mean they all vote Conservative. One stood as a Liberal candidate in another constituency, to the indignation of his neighbours. Some of the smaller farmers are thought to vote Labour and to join the U.A. to hide the fact, through fear of the comments of class peers should their allegiance become known. This at least indicates that middle class people expect each other to vote Conservative. Even if they all do, there is a marked difference in emphasis among them between those who have always been property owners and those who are or have been in the professions. Though both share attitudes not found in the working class, for example, that the character of a politician in terms of fair-mindedness and wartime activities is more important than his ideas, the professional men have no ideological hostility to the Welfare State whereas the others have.

The former tend to see political problems as only problems of administration.

These inadequate observations show two structural features which seem to be general, viz., that on any issue the working class is sharply divided while the middle classes are more unanimous, though with a difference of emphasis between property owners and professionals. For example, attitudes to the modern system of education show these features, the issue being the sending of parish children to town schools at the age of thirteen. Farmers are indignant about this, the upper-middle class more so, even though their own children are schooled outside the parish, holding that working class children do not need any schooling after thirteen and don't benefit from it. They also claim that the experience children get of town life makes them reject the country; it is responsible for 'rural depopulation'. The professional people agree there is some substance to this but have reservations – they hold all children should attend secondary school so that the few who might benefit will have the chance to do so.

The working class is sharply divided on the matter. The majority, while having no special regard for secondary education, hold that working class children should have the same opportunities as others. As for the farmers' objection that sending them to town schools contributes to rural depopulation, they sneer and accuse the farmers of 'thinking only of themselves', of wanting to ensure a supply of labour. Yet a large minority agree on every point with the farmers, saying most of the children are 'duds' anyway and that it is a waste of time and money sending them for two years to secondary school.

This structure is also seen in attitudes to the history of the parish described earlier. For the middle classes this has been a record of a change from a good to a bad state of affairs. The handing over of local administration entirely to paid bureaucrats has been a mistake; they are not in touch with local opinion and needs. State authorized regulation of conditions of farm work has reduced productivity and caused resentment between master and servant as farm work cannot be satisfactorily done to a routine but is now forced into one. Workmen no longer work so hard and there is too much travelling into town by workmen and their wives, causing discontentment, especially among the latter. The professionals again have reservations – that administration now must plan for far larger units than the parish if it is to be effective, for example. Some maintain that the agricultural labourer was underpaid formerly, though they regret that it was a union which won increases for them.

An opposite evaluation is held by the majority of the working class. Life has improved, farmers are just as mean as ever but are now forced to pay a more reasonable wage and can't make you slave from dawn to dusk. They have a joke, one of their traditional stock, to illustrate this change. A farmer in the district once made his men work from five in the morning till half past ten at night then told them they could go to bed, adding that bed was the best thing in life. A shepherd retorted that it wasn't such a good thing as darkness for without darkness they would never get to bed. 'They can't do that now' workmen exult. Moreover life in the country is more bearable now, especially for wives, because it is easier to get to town. A minority however takes much the same view as the farmer, though not entirely for the same reasons. Most of this minority are people aged forty and above, and they maintain that formerly people were much happier. A few say that despite higher wages their standard of living is no higher, as proof of which they say that formerly it was possible to save money whereas now it is not. Those holding these opinions usually also regret that the real 'gentlemen', i.e., 'the county' have departed; they ran the farms and the parish with efficiency and justice and without the snobbery so characteristic of the present big farmers.

All the outward features of culture mentioned play an important part in the system of relations in the parish, for almost any distinctive feature of a class becomes a symbol of it. 'Cottager' for example is a polite synonym for 'working class person'. All informants agreed that speech and accent were the most trustworthy symbols in placing a stranger, with clothes and manners a fairly reliable second. That all these function as symbols of status is clearly seen in the treatment meted out to persons who attempt to display one of these traits as it is displayed by a class higher than the one they are known to belong to. They are ridiculed in a way which shows that they are held to be trying to claim a class status they are not entitled to. For example, recently some working youths bought a suit of clothing of the expensive sort worn in the upper-middle class. They were jeered at by their class peers and each given a nickname showing he was regarded as claiming illegitimate status – 'Lord Westrigg', 'Sir X', and so on. Similarly there is one working class family whose speech is more like the middle classes than like the rest of the working class. The lower-middle class regarded this family with approval saying they did not speak so 'Scotch' as the others and were not 'rough' in manner, etc. To the rest of the working class the family is 'affected', accused of 'putting on airs' and 'thinking itself above us'.

Another indication of the importance of these cultural features as status symbols is that they are sometimes used by a person of low status to compel favourable treatment from one of high status. In this situation the latter has to be ignorant of the true position of the former. A forestry foreman, new to the district, a widely travelled and sophisticated person, tells how he dealt in this way with an upper-middle class farmer who wanted advice about planting trees. . . 'I knew if he knew I was only a foreman he'd treat me like dirt so I wore my hat and raincoat when I went up to see him. He was a bit puzzled at first, you could see it in his face – he'd been expecting someone he could boss around, but I just looked knowledgeable and talked in a big way about this and that – put on an accent a bit and so on. So he thawed down gradually, treated me as an equal anyway.'

So far I have treated culture as a set of symbols announcing class status. Two observations are appropriate here. One is that the items of culture which can be viewed in this way seem practically endless. Once, when discussing status symbols with a craftsman's apprentice he claimed to be able to spot any upper-middle class stranger as such. Asked how, he replied – 'anything about them tells you, why they look as if they owned the bloody world.' In view of the figures showing acreages owned by the classes (page 79), this is hardly surprising. Several people remarked that you could easily distinguish them even at a distance because they walked 'as if they thought they were important.' Some pointed out you could easily distinguish farmers from shepherds by their different ways of using the walking stick – the farmer 'flicking it into the air', the latter using it actually to assist walking.

The other observation is that the possibility of viewing culture in this way does not exhaust its reality. It is merely one attitude among others which a person can adopt towards another and in no way absolves him from behaving as a member of his class or of experiencing class culture in other ways.

For example, the culture of the higher classes is officially defined as better than that of the lower. In the local school the language and manners taught are those of the middle classes. Though the majority of the children are of the working class they are discouraged from using their own normal speech. During one lesson, for example, the children were asked to name various sorts of buildings shown to them in pictures, of which one was a kennel. Asked to name it one of the boys replied correctly in dialect 'a dughoose'. He was somewhat chagrined to be told he was 'wrong'. In short the children are being trained to believe that their normal way of speaking is wrong and to imitate the dialect of the middle classes. The same applies to manners; the children are taught to address and refer to adults as 'Mr' and 'Mrs', to use handkerchiefs and to be circumspect in interaction with others. These are middle class customs. Working class men in particular demand of each other an immediate solidarity in interaction which seems to render middle class manners superfluous.

This brief sketch of class cultures I hope justifies the use of the term 'social milieu' to describe the nature of social class. A social class is neither a mere category arbitrarily defined by myself on the basis of one or two 'characteristics' such as property ownership, nor is it a group in the strict sense of the term as implying clear cut boundaries and a constitution laying down a limited set of relationships among its members. A class is rather, for its members, one of the major horizons of all social experience, an area within which most experience is defined. Encompassing so much, it is rarely conceptualized. In the previous chapter I mentioned (page 99) a pervasive indefiniteness in the system due to different classes stressing different values as crucial in estimating relative prestige. Another pervasive indefiniteness of the same sort arises from the fact that parishioners rarely conceptualize it. As the Table of Class Placements makes clear, there is no common conception of a 'class system' among parishioners. While everyone is aware that people are of high and low status and there is general agreement on the ordering of families in this way, one woman, for example, thought there were seven social classes while one man thought there were only two. This lack of concensus has no special explanation apart from the features of the system discussed in the last chapter unless it is the fact that the whole subject is taboo in conversation. While terms like 'working folk' or 'gentleman farmer' crop up spontaneously in conversation the concepts are never critically discussed.

This does not mean that the concept of a local class system is a sociologist's myth; it only means that individuals, when asked about it, answer in terms of their own experience of it. That there is a system is I think shown by the fact that no informant placed him or herself wrongly, no one claimed a status higher or lower than that accorded by the majority of fellow parishioners. Each person knows his or her place in the system, can place accurately other people he has the requisite information about, but has no need to turn his experience of the system into a conceptual scheme. Apart from the structured perspectives described (page 99), individuals differ in the extent to which they objectify the system, and some perhaps suffer or ignore it rather than objectify it.[1] Two male parishioners, for example, refused to make class placements for me, one on the grounds that there was 'something invidious about classifying people in that way', another because it 'wasn't nice'. As the words indicate the former was an upper-middle class, the latter a working class man, but both seemed to be saying the same thing. Two women (both working class) on the other hand thanked me for the interview and discussion, one, because 'it does you good to get it off your chest', the other, because 'I've never talked about these things before.'

I have the impression that the higher the class the more numerous are individuals who can objectify the system, and that the lower the class the more it approximates a total social milieu for its members (though it can never be completely so, and those individuals described on page 106 are impressive exceptions).[2] This would not be surprising in view of the restricted participa-

---

[1] For an interesting analysis of differences between American social classes in ability to objectify events, see L. Schatzman and A. Strauss, 'Social Class and Modes of Communication', *Amer. Jour. Soc.*, Vol. 60, No. 4, pages 329–38.

[2] An extended description of working class culture as a total social milieu is given by R. Hoggart, *The Uses of Literacy*, Chatto & Windus, 1957.

tion of the working class in the wider network of relationships described below (page 114 ff.). It is also perhaps apparent from the number of devices the working class employ to dull the force of the invidious comparisons latent in the system, though the existence of these devices is a recognition of that invidiousness. A common belief among working men and especially shepherds is that they 'keep the boss right', i.e., prevent the stock on a farm from degenerating by giving sound advice to the farmer who otherwise by ignorant breeding policies would ruin it. Most farmers are willing to listen to the advice of a trusted shepherd, but are annoyed to hear them claiming more. Another belief is that riches can only be got or possessed at the cost of happiness, hence the poor are happier than the rich. There is of course no contradiction in an individual expressing superiority at one moment and envy at another (as they sometimes do), the moments being separate in time; rather is it an honesty in face of the ambiguity of (almost) total life situations, such as membership of a social class. Searching for a meaning in them (the situations), the individual finds he can interpret them in various ways which shift with his own moods. A final example – working class women in the context of serving food (see page 128) often by some remark emphasize the homeliness of the arrangements they make; though there may be no direct reference to the way middle class women behave in the same context, it is clear from the tone of voice used that the working class women are attempting to confer some magical virtue on homeliness as against the artificiality they perceive in the middle class female's arrangements. As to how far anyone 'believes' the judgment implicit in such remarks – that would require some notion of what belief is; the remarks initiate a movement towards an immediate solidarity in face of the possiblities of comparison, and succeed in that aim. But how the possibilities of comparison are to be dealt with is finally an individual matter, revealing as much about the individual as about the class system.

CHAPTER VII

CLASS AND SOCIAL ORGANIZATION

Class and the wider society

THE classes differ in the range and frequency of their association outside the parish. The norm here is that the higher a class the wider and more frequent are its contacts outside the parish; or to adopt the network image used in Chapter IV, the higher the class the more dispersed is the network of relationships in which it is involved, the lower the class the more contained is its network.[1] The basis of the difference in scale is the former's relative freedom from having to work to a routine timetable, and ownership of private means of transport and communication, as opposed to the latter's being tied to a daily job and dependent on public transport.

The difference between classes in scale of networks of outside contact has already been indicated on page 97, where I showed that kinship connections within the parish were more frequent among working and lower-middle class than among upper-middle class persons. Many other data can be cited to support the generalization.

Some men of all classes belong to a Masonic Lodge in Broadfield and to the Broadfield branch of the British Legion. Members of the lower middle and working classes belong to a unit of the Observer Corps which has its H.Q. in England. This rarely takes them outside the parish. Members of all classes are in their appropriate Unions and sometimes attend branch meetings in Broadfield or Craigton. This defines the extent of working and lower-middle class participation in formal associations outside the parish. The upper-middle class participate more regularly

---

[1] The terms 'dispersed' and 'contained network' are borrowed from W. Watson. See W. Watson and M. Susser, *op. cit.*

in associations further afield. Several belong to a bridge club which meets once a week in winter months in a town 25 miles away. A few belong to men's clubs in Edinburgh. One belongs to a society with headquarters in London whose exhibitions he attends. Regular contact with official bodies outside the parish is much more frequent among this class than is the case with the other two. The elected representative of the parish on the County Council has been for two generations a member of this class: the representative on the District Council also. Two of them are members of a Committee set up by the Department of Agriculture for Scotland. Another is on the Committee of a Missionary Society. The women of this class too are found on official bodies whose range is wider than the parish – County or District Committees of, for example, the W.R.I. (Womens Rural Institute), or the Brownies. From time to time one or other of them accepts office in some outside body. Members of the other two classes are rarely members of such committees.

Both in formal and informal association distance is not very much of a barrier to the upper-middle class in pursuit of professional or recreational interests. Several attend from time to time lectures on agricultural topics in Edinburgh, a few attend critical meetings of the Farmers' Union in London or Edinburgh. From time to time one of them becomes interested in promoting the breeding and diffusion of a particular type of animal, travels to markets throughout the country and perhaps becomes a judge of such stock at exhibitions and markets everywhere. Even as regards domicile this class is not limited to the parish, one farming family living the cold half of the year in a nearby town and the summer months in Westrigg. A few regularly attend social functions in Edinburgh, garden parties, balls, and so forth, and one or two travel up to visit a concert or a play during the Festival. The notable drinkers of this class sometimes disappear for several days at a time. Disdain for the impediments of distance was recently carried to its extreme by one farmer who is a member of the local hunt. The hunt seemed about to disband through various difficulties, but he declared that the prospect did not dismay him for he would fly over to Ireland once a week and hunt there.

The classes differ in their practices with regard to holidays. Working class children are often during the school summer holidays sent to live with grandparents in some nearby parish or town. Working class adults rarely have a holiday in the sense of spending several consecutive days living somewhere else. Though all employed males are entitled to so many holidays with pay, agricultural workers rarely have more than one day off work at a time, during which they go no further than some nearby town. Forestry workers have ten consecutive days holiday, usually spent at home or living with relatives in nearby parishes and towns. There are of course exceptions to this general pattern in the working class, particularly among the youths. Every year three of four go to some recognized holiday place such as the Isle of Man.

Among the lower-middle class holidays are much the same as in the working class, at least among farming families. They are rarely away from the farm for more than a day at a time. However, they get away oftener than the majority of working people, and possessing cars they can get away whenever they feel like it, not on Saturdays only, as is the case with those dependent on public transport. They seem to range wider in their contacts outside the parish than the working class, being familiar with the topography of either Glasgow or Edinburgh.

Members of the upper-middle class usually take holidays every year, spend a week or a fortnight living outside the parish – sometimes longer. They go farther afield than any other classes – London, Ireland or the Continent. In the course of their lives they visit parts of the world the other classes see, if at all, only as members of Her Majesty's Forces. The two ex-colonial civil servants have of course lived in various places in the colonies in the course of their former duties. In addition members of this class have visited, at their own expense, such countries as America, Canada, the Argentine, Scandinavia, Austria. The difference between the children of this class and of the other two with regard to schooling has already been mentioned.

At this point it may be asked whether in fact the middle classes have lost power in the parish over the last fifty years. As far as I could determine, representatives of the country parish on official bodies whose transactions affect the lives of parishioners are almost all of the upper-middle class. Yet the middle classes are by no means dominant on, for example, the County Council. Many of the representatives of burghs and towns on it are of the working class. Moreover the greater part of the work of the Council is done by salaried bureaucrats whose main interest is simply to supply services as efficiently as possible. These matters require more investigation than I could devote to them. The data, however, suggests that the more frequent contacts, both formal and informal, of the upper-middle class outside the parish serve to maintain their position of dominance within the parish.[1]

Family, Marriage and Class

It is the family and not the individual that is the unit of social class.[2] By family in this context I mean those members of a family living together in the same household. It is necessary to state this because an individual can alter his class status in his own lifetime (see below); the child can come to occupy a different status from his parents, the sibling from the sibling. In such cases persons of different status do not live together as members of the same household. That the family, in this sense, is the unit was clear both from informants, class placements and their comments while making them. In no instance were children separated from parents or husband from wife. One informant simply ranked the men and remarked that 'wives and children just go with the head of the house.' In their comments they rarely mentioned an individual's name, but spoke of the 'the X's' – the whole family. Children inherit a class status, some inherit an occupation, and the family as a whole shares the symbols of class status.

Occupation is an important factor determining class status. In this community some occupations are very much bound up with family membership. Of the ten farmers resident in the parish seven are sons of farmers; all shepherds are the sons of shepherds.[3] This does not mean that a person's occupation is determined by his membership of a family. A sample of sixteen shepherds in the parish have thirty-three brothers employed elsewhere of whom seventeen are also shepherds, i.e., two out of

[1] See on this W. Goldschmidt, *Social Class in America*, Amer. Anthrop., Vol. 52, 1950, pp. 483-498.

[2] See H. M. Johnson, *op. cit.*, page 470.

[3] It is unlikely that all shepherds everywhere in the country are sons of shepherds, yet instances where they are not seem to be comparatively rare.

three shepherds' sons are shepherds. Similarly, not all farmers' sons are farmers. A relation between family and occupation holds to any significant degree only in these two occupations, the connection in both cases being the institution of inheritance. In the one case farms are inherited, in the other skills. The seven farmers mentioned all inherited their farms while the shepherds all learned the elements of their craft from their fathers. Many of the skills of shepherding such as identifying illness among sheep or knowing when to move them to another pasture require instruction and a certain amount of practice. As no institution teaches them they have to be learned on the job. In the case of the other agricultural occupations there is no such direct link with the family, though the fathers of the general agricultural workers all followed some rural occupation themselves.

A family shares many of the symbols of class status, and much of the behaviour which goes to make up a class culture is taught in the family, for example manners, dialect, form and content of conversation. A middle class mother remarked 'I was always afraid that (my children) would pick up the accent of the cottagers from the other children at school, but they didn't, they speak like us.' She went on to say that her children often pointed out differences in behaviour between themselves and working class children and asked the reason for them, and added 'I didn't want them to be snobbish but I always said something to make them see that our ways are best.'

The house, standard of living and eating customs are shared by a family and are important status symbols. The main index parishioners use in deciding what class a family belongs to is who it associates closely with, and this is decided by considering whose house members of the family can enter and eat food in. Here as elsewhere throughout the world commensality symbolizes close relations between those eating together.[1] Whenever I asked a working class informant why he placed someone in the middle class the first response was 'because he wouldn't come in here and have a cup of tea', often with the addition 'I wouldn't ask him and he wouldn't ask me.' An upper-middle class farmer told how when he first started farming he would sometimes have his midday meal outside with the men, 'however, I noticed my being there put a damper on the conversation and it was very uncom-

[1] See e.g. A. R. Radcliffe-Brown, *The Andaman Islanders*, Cambridge, 1933.

fortable, so I stopped it.' As he was not in fact in a close relation with his men, to eat with them merely impugned the value of the symbol, a situation which invariably causes discomfort.

The importance of entering the house as an index of close relations kept cropping up in all interviews. One elderly working man maintained that class barriers are less rigorous now than in his youth because formerly he was never allowed inside a middle class house whereas now when on business visits 'I'm sometimes allowed as far as the kitchen'. An upper-middle class woman boasted that her husband had occasionally been invited to a shooting party by the 'county lot', implying that he was a close associate of them. He deflated her with, 'yes, but I'm never asked in' (to the house). It is for this reason that several informants found it difficult to place the minister, since as they said, he visits everyone. However they drew a distinction between duty visits and visits from choice in his case. It is sharing the house and food of families other than one's own that constitutes the exemplary type of association that most unambiguously fixes class membership.

Since a family begins with a marriage, and since a class system restricts association among the population stratified, a full account of the connections between family and class must deal with the process known as assortative mating.[1] Social barriers of any sort limit the possibilities of random contact among people, and tend to foster marriages between persons with similar social characteristics. Social class barriers are among the most important in this process. Where a class system prevails there are three possible combinations of class status of the spouses. The two can be of equal status, the man higher than the woman or the woman higher than the man. The first combination is the normal one; of all marriages in the parish only eight were not of this sort.[2] The second combination is much more frequent than the third, the ratio here being seven to one.[3]

[1] On assortative mating see D. V. Glass (ed.), *op. cit.*, and W. Watson and M. Susser, *op. cit.*

[2] For a statistical treatment of this subject see D. V. Glass (ed.), *op. cit.* Also S. M. Lipset, *Social Mobility in Industrial Society*, University of California, 1959.

[3] In these observations on assortative mating, I have considered mobility by reference to the status of the father of the parties to marriage.

Where the spouses are not equal in status the woman has con-
ferred upon her the class status of the man. When making class
placements informants never separated husband and wife, but
also in comments on the status of the family it was always
attributes of the male head which were cited – his possessions,
education and so forth. Where the woman marries a man
of higher status she is accepted as an associate by wives of the
husband's class peers, though if the status gap between the two
is a wide one – spans more than one class barrier – there may be
a transition period for the woman in which she is, as it were, on
trial before being accepted. Thus in one case of this sort in which
the wife was a complete stranger to the parishioners, it was, as an
informant put it, 'touch and go' whether or not the upper-middle
class women of the parish would associate with her. At that time
the women of this class had a sort of social leader, a woman of
strong character whose judgments on all sorts of matters were
accepted by the rest. After the new wife had visited her several
times the leader decided to accept her as an associate and the
others followed suit. The wife is well aware of the issues the
marriage created for her husband. Once when he complained of
being unable to win a position of any influence in local politics
she remarked, 'that's because you married me', an explanation
her husband rejected.

In that combination there is no loss of status but a gain for the
woman. On the other hand, where a man of lower status marries
a woman of higher, there is no gain but a loss for the woman.[1]
In one marriage of this sort the wife was a daughter of a farmer
in another parish, her husband a farm worker. She never associated with the lower-middle class women of the parish but with
the wives of other farm workers, among whom she was very
popular.

Parents try to prevent daughters making such a match. One
middle class girl said, 'my parents have always been against (my
fiancée) from the beginning. It's just because he's a cottager.
They've always tried to prevent us having anything to do with
cottagers. They used to stop us going to dances round about; we
used to have to creep out the house when they were asleep if we
wanted to go to them. But they've always . . . mother especially

[1] It is possible, of course, that this does not apply with regard to other
social classes than those found in Westrigg.

... tried to turn me against (my fiancée). I always said "if he was a farmer's son you wouldn't find anything wrong with him".' She also remarked that she knew that many of her friends would drop her if she married him but added 'I'll find out who my real friends are.' Further interview material showing active parental opposition to this kind of match is presented below.

Why this type of combination is so rare is discussed below; meanwhile it may be asked why any sort of marriage across class lines is relatively rare. Numerous reasons can be adduced which, however, are merely implicit in the class system itself. For example, members of a class associate by choice with each other rather than with those of a class lower down, so that the chances of intimate association between members of different classes are few. Secondly, members of a higher class regard those of a lower as in some sense inferior to themselves. The attitude varies in degree in different individuals, but is still common to all members of a class. When cross-class marriage or courtship does occur it is usual to find the higher partner claiming that the spouse is an exception to the general run of his or her class. The attitude must form an initial barrier to intimate association. Finally the different cultures of the classes may also form barriers. Most informants could cite a case of cross class marriage which turned out to be 'difficult' for this reason, the couple constantly quarrelling over, e.g., the education of the children. Whether or not the marriages cited were 'difficult' for that reason cannot be said, but it is clear that the majority of people believe that there is a difficulty here which has to be overcome.

These 'reasons' are however only aspects of the class system itself. Perhaps a more cogent explanation is to be found in the incompatability between kinship norms and those governing relations between classes. There is a warm and friendly relationship between grandparents and children, and between parent's siblings and sibling's children. In cross-class marriage the children are in a different class from the parents and siblings of one of the spouses. People of different classes do not associate in warm friendly relations. It seems likely that if marriage between members of different classes became general either the kinship system or the class system would have to alter very much from their present form. While I have not data to prove this, it is clear that in the community there is incompatability between the two sets of norms and that where they conflict class norms take precedence. Relations with kinsfolk of a lower class are either severed or become characterized by a certain reserve. In either case accusations of snobbery are made by the lower against the higher. For example, one lower-middle class man has an uncle in the parish who is a farm worker, but the two never associate. The former and his wife regard the latter as a tiresome old man, though he is highly respected among the working class. The uncle and members of his household sometimes express resentment against the nephew and his household.

That too frequent marriage across class lines might destroy the present class system is suggested by the fact that marriage of a woman of higher status to a man of lower is very much rarer than the opposite. It is regarded as a more serious breach of the norm. Rees remarks on this in the Welsh parish too, that 'the marriage of a farmer's daughter to a labourer is a more serious matter, sometimes leading to lasting estrangement'.[1] In this case there is a loss of status for the women, and were her parents to maintain normal relations with her children they would share in the loss of status through association with them. Association outside of work relationships (as already described) is not merely a sociologist's index of equality of status; it is what equality of status means in everyday behaviour in the community itself. To put it in an abstract way – society has a limited stock of status to distribute, each family being guardian of a certain amount according to its position in the class system. If women commonly married men of lower status, either this total stock would be dissipated by the normal association among kinsfolk, or else there would be 'lasting estrangements' i.e., kinship relations entirely destroyed.

Class and sex roles

The sexes are allotted different roles and how these articulate with the class system is the theme of this section. The division of labour between them is the same in this community as in the rest of the nation: after marriage men are gainfully employed while women work in the house and tend the children. This division of labour is probably more marked in rural society than

[1] A. D. Rees, *op. cit.*, page 146.

it is in many areas of industrial society, for obvious reasons – lack of light employment, of transport and so on. No extended description of it is given here as it is common knowledge.

That the sexes stand in different relationships to the class system is clear from differential rates of social mobility. Of the present agricultural population of the parish and its siblings who live outside, twenty have in their own lifetime moved up a class, of whom fourteen are women and six men.[1] All but one of these have moved from the working into the lower-middle class; accordingly this analysis refers to these two classes – movement from one to the other and from the working class into the 'slum class' below it.

Because a woman's status derives from that of a man it might seem as if the wife and mother had no responsibility for the status of the family. In the working class this is not the case. The wife can have no responsibility for gaining status for her family but she has a great deal of responsibility for maintaining its status and can be responsible for its downfall into the non-respectable 'slum class'. A consideration of the criteria which mark off the two classes makes this clear, for the differences between them concern only household economy, which is largely the wives' affair.[2] In the working class the family is expected to use a tablecloth or oilcloth and not always eat off bare boards; to use earthenware and china dishes and not enamelled tin ones; to have at least one cooked meal a day; to have a clean outfit of clothes for public appearances; and not to get into debt with tradesmen. The children's school clothes should not fall below a certain standard of cleanliness and neatness, nor should the material apparatus of the household.

It is failure to maintain these standards which alone distinguishes the non-respectable 'slum class' from the working class. I have not considered this class as part of the structure of the community because often there are no representatives of it present and there are never more than one or two families when they do appear (see page 73). However, here is an example of the way such a family is talked of by its respectable neighbours in

[1] Figures on comparative rates of social mobility in various countries are to be found in B. Barber, *op. cit.*, pages 422–477.

[2] This seems to be the case also in America. See A. Davis, B. B. Gardener and M. B. Gardner, *Deep South*, Chicago, 1941.

Westrigg. 'He was a nice fellow . . . but she was an awful creature. They left as she owed too much all round . . . she used to be after everybody here. She'd ask for anything – clothes, money, food . . . she used to send the bairns for them . . . oh it was terrible, every time you looked out the window and saw one of the bairns you sat quaking. She never cooked anything. . . bread and jam it was, just bread and jam.' The informant went on to describe how everyone tried to avoid contact with the wife. Responsibility for the downfall of the family was fixed on her by the neighbours through criteria known to them all. The husband earned as much as the other labourers and was moderate in his own personal consumption; the neighbours reckoned that it was her expenditure on cigarettes and beer for herself that left the family so badly equipped. Whether or not it is actually always the woman who is responsible for this downward mobility is irrelevant here; it is the female role which is being analysed.

On the other hand, the woman has no responsibility for gaining status for the total family. The labourer or shepherd must become a farmer, or the forestry labourer a manager. That these moves are extremely difficult for a workman to make has some bearing on differential mobility rates. To become a farmer requires capital which could never be saved from a married workman's wage. As for loans, a local bank manager pointed out that the price of farms and stock has risen so much in the last few decades that it is virtually impossible for a farm labourer to acquire a farm. A forestry worker has to recommend himself to the manager by hard work, skill and by showing a capacity for command. If accepted in a forestry school and successful in its examinations he may leave it as a foreman and perhaps in time be promoted to manager. The age limit for entry to the school is twenty-five. It is most unusual for a workman to display a capacity for command since his workmates resent it in anyone not a manager. The only other way of moving into the middle class is to migrate to a town or a dominion and change occupation altogether. (This in fact is what all the successfully mobile men have done, though all but one did so before marriage.)[1]

[1] I refrain from giving short biographies of individuals in this book as I have no wish to embarrass any of the many parishioners who helped me in this study.

Whatever the difficulties, these moves can only be made by the male.

Consideration of the movement of single persons brings out other aspects of the different relationships of the sexes to the class system. Most upward movement is accomplished before marriage, by the act of marriage itself, or else the first steps such as acquiring an education are taken before it. Since upward movement is more difficult after marriage and also thereafter depends upon the male, marriage for the female is a crucial choice as regards class status. She cannot by her own efforts gain further status, only maintain or lose it. Of the fourteen women who moved up eight did so by the act of marriage, by marrying a man of higher status, and six by acquiring an education which entitled them to middle class jobs. Of these latter two consolidated their position by marriage. It is clear that the roles allotted the sexes in the working class favour mobility in the female.

The female role contains skills which within the present structure of rural society provides better opportunity for upward mobility. Her main skills in the first place are portable (i.e., can be carried from one area of society to another, in this case from one class to another).[1] Housekeeping differs only in scale, if at all, from working to lower-middle class, and as far as I could observe child rearing techniques do not differ greatly.[2] Her other skills, in adornment, charm and manners are not only portable but also are social techniques enabling the manipulation of others and fostering an insight into social relations. All these skills are important in achieving her main objective in upward movement (marriage). The male role, on the other hand, is heavily loaded with occupational skills which are either not portable or are so only within one occupational hierarchy. No amount of development of these skills by themselves, however, facilitates mobility – e.g. an expert shepherd does not in any

[1] An object, skill, person or quality is portable when it, he or she can be carried from one area of society to another without prejudice to the person moving. Symbols of class status are non-portable, or pigmentation where a colour-bar is enforced.

[2] Opportunities to observe child rearing techniques were however somewhat limited, and it may be that there are differences between the two classes in this respect. Difference in this area however would I imagine, as with other cultural differences, be characterized by gradual alteration rather than sudden mutation.

way increase his chances of becoming a farmer by his efficiency. A full understanding of this situation requires further analysis of the structure of rural society.

One structural element that is important here is the relation between the sexes in the working class. Though there are exceptions to the generalization (see page 135), dominance of the male and distance between the sexes are the outstanding characteristics of the relationship. In general in this class system the higher the class the less dominant the male and the less distance between the sexes. The distance is very apparent in the working class, permitting a wide divergence of culture between the sexes.[1] It is perhaps most clearly seen in recreation. Three voluntary associations draw their membership mainly from the working class – the bowling club, the W.R.I., and the church guild. The first is exclusively male the other two exclusively female. The other two associations, a badminton and a drama club, recruit from both lower middle and working class and both sexes of the middle class participate in them, but not both sexes of the working class. While dancing and courtship naturally require participation by both sexes, the pattern for the married and those past youth on visits to town on Saturday is for the men to spend the evening in pubs and women at the cinema or visiting relatives. In the lower-middle class both sexes participate together in many recreations, for example in addition to those mentioned, motoring and picturegoing, and in the upper middle in most recreations – bridge, dinner parties, travel, etc. In reading matter the same distance is found. The basic pattern for the working class is that men read Westerns, thrillers and technical magazines on farming, while women read romances and technical magazines on housekeeping. There are of course common daily and weekly papers, and sometimes magazines designed for both sexes are found in working class homes. Magazines and books read by both sexes increase the higher the class though each sex still has its own technical magazines. An interesting example is car driving. In

---

[1] This seems to be a feature of American class systems also. W. L. Warner and P. S. Lunt, *op. cit.*, remark (page 119) 'Sexual solidarities are very strong in the lower group.' See also W. B. Miller, 'Implication of Urban lower class culture for social work', *Soc. Serv. Rev.*, Vol. 33, No. 3, pages 219–36; and H. Johnson, *op. cit.*, pages 472–74.

the working class it is rare to find a woman who drives (i.e., in those families possessing a car); in the lower-middle class it is less rare, but female drivers are less skilled than male; most upper-middle class females drive and are as expert as the males. The distance between the sexes in the working class is aptly indicated in terms of reference used by husband and wife. He refers to her as 'she', or 'the wife', and she refers to him as 'my man', or 'the man', and sometimes 'he'.

Within the working class, male dominance is exemplified in numerous details of social life. For example, husbands sometimes censure wives in front of children. Visitors in a working class house are usually offered the fireside chair the wife normally occupies while the husband stays put in his. If other men are in the house, the wife must either remain silent or join in the men's conversation which always centres round male topics, particularly work, sport, politics or personal history. In the middle class male dominance in everyday life is less apparent, and in the upper-middle class deference is accorded the female by the male. He will stand aside to let her go through doorways first, will rise when she enters the room and give her his seat and so on. Conversation can be initiated by women about prices, babies, etc. (or about such topics as politics, economic conditions, etc., which in the other classes are 'male' topics) in which men join in, and women have a large say in many spheres of family life, particularly in the education of children.[1]

The higher position of the wife in the middle class household *vis-à-vis* the husband is expressed in the ceremony surrounding meals, particularly tea, a meal at which all members of the family in all classes are usually present. There is a marked difference between the working class on the one hand and the two middle classes on the other in the way behaviour is patterned during the meal, a difference which aptly expresses the difference in status of the wife in the two sorts of household.

In the upper-middle class where a whole family is present at tea everyone sits down at the table together, including the housewife. At her side are the teapot, milk jug, sugar bowl and all the cups. She knows the tastes of the members of her family and

---

[1] Amongst the working class, education of the children is rarely discussed and, except perhaps in some cases of inter-class marriage, is not something that either spouse feels he or she has to have the final say about.

hands each a complete cup of tea, milk and sugar, ready for drinking. Each says 'thank you' as she hands it to them.

Should a visitor be present she asks him if he takes milk. If he does she adds it to the tea she has poured into his cup, then asks him if he takes sugar and adds it if he does. To her queries the visitor has to respond with 'yes please' or 'no thank you'. During the course of the meal the wife keeps asking everyone if they would like another cup of tea. Also during the course of the meal she has to keep offering everyone things to eat. It is considered bad manners for a visitor to help himself to any food on the table. Even if he wanted to however he would hardly get the opportunity to do so, for the wife is quick to invite him to eat something else as soon as he has finished some little morsel of food. Members of the family are also invited by the wife to eat; they do not have to wait for her to offer the food but if they want some they have to ask for it, adding 'please', or saying 'pass me (something), please'. The food itself is so arranged as to facilitate these operations of the wife – bread is cut thin, often made into minute sandwiches, scones are small, and large cakes are put on the table uncut so that if anyone wants a piece of cake he or she can only have it after the housewife has specially cut a piece for him. All this ceremony emphasizes the control the housewife has over food. One gets food by virtue of her kindness.[1]

At the working class table arrangements and behaviour are very different. Usually each person has an empty cup set beside his plate. The housewife walks round the table pouring tea into these cups before she sits down. Sometimes she has the cups beside her, as in the middle class arrangement, and sends out a cup containing only tea to each person. Whatever the exact arrangement here, each person gets a cup containing only tea. Milk and sugar are in the centre of the table and each person simply reaches out his hand for them and adds them as he wishes to his cup. Food is in the centre of the table too and each person reaches out his hand and takes what he wants, without reference to the wife or anyone else. If some plate of food is beyond arm's reach, one takes one's knife and stabs the desired item on the

[1] W. L. Warner and P. S. Lunt, *op. cit.*, page 106, remark that 'These ritual elements surrounding the daily life within a household tend to increase in number and intensity of function with the height of the stratification of the family.

plate and brings it onto one's own plate. A visitor is told to 'help yourself' or 'put out your hand and reach' and the wife never offers him anything until he shows signs of stopping eating altogether. The food is again arranged specifically to fit into this pattern of activity – bread is cut thick and is never made into sandwiches, scones are large, and cakes are put on the table already cut into pieces. If one wants more tea one simply passes one's cup to the housewife, without using any words. Often, however, she rises and brings the teapot to one, as soon as she sees that one's cup is empty. In other words the wife here has no control over the food but instead performs a servant-like role during the meal.

Turning now from status within the family to esteem, i.e., reputation for efficient performance of one's role, a disparity between male and female roles appears which is independent of class position. The reputation a man can win in his occupational role ranges much further than a woman can win in hers. A farmer can become known even in the Dominions as a good stocksman, a shepherd can become known to his fellows throughout Britain as an excellent craftsman, but no woman can become so widely famous as a good wife, mother and housekeeper. On a purely local level the disparity appears partly as one of intensity. Woman's work is not publicly judged and priced every year as the man's is at the lamb and tup sales. It is true that there are fêtes organized by the W.R.I. or Church Guild in which competitions in baking, sewing, the 'bonniest baby', etc. feature, but these as well as being confined to a parish or district never arouse so much excitement and comment as the yearly sales. These competitions are moreover voluntary and most women do not regard participating in them as competition so much as simply contributing to the activities of the club, while the men's work is annually displayed and judged whether they like it or not. Even in everyday conversation men are constantly being judged as good or bad farmers, shepherds, etc., while women are less often and with less fine discrimination so judged. In short men are heavily involved in an esteem system while the women are not.

In the working class the women perform their role without public comment as efficiently as is required to maintain the standing of the family, and failing that, they take the family down into the 'slum class'. The dominance of the male implies that the men can win greater esteem than the women. Women are publicly proud of any outstanding achievement of their husbands (e.g. breeding a prize-winning animal) while men do not exhibit publicly any pride in an outstanding achievement of their wives. Women acquiesce in the implicit evaluation here, that their role requires less skill than the men's. The odd male who develops some household skill like baking is disparagingly called a 'Jessie' by both sexes; a man who chatters is contemptuously called a sweetiewife' by both sexes. On the other hand a woman who develops a male skill as, for example, in handling dogs is admired for it.[1]

Barred from winning wide esteem, the women tend to focus their interest on status.[2] The different orientation of the sexes is clearly reflected in their reading matter. The men's stories, Westerns and thrillers, are all action and no social structure – the heroes perform super-efficiently and that is all. Many of the women's stories on the other hand are all about social structure and how to deal with it. Their favourite magazine is the *People's Friend* in which the stories are mainly about marriage and kinship and about social class. One year, for example, two serials in it told, in the one, of how a working class girl married an upper-middle class man, and in the other, how a working class mother pushed her children into the middle class through insisting they stay at school, etc. Class structure in these stories is taken for granted and situations built around it. More direct indication of the women's interest in status, and of the importance of marriage in her status gaining behaviour can be found; for example, all the publicly identified 'social climbers' in the community are women. (By publicly identified I mean a wide range of people so identified them to me.) Or here is one wife – 'I didn't want to marry a working man, I wanted one with clean hands, but I got landed with (my baby). My sister laughed at me when

[1] There was one woman in the parish good at handling dogs and capable of performing all the duties of a shepherd. Several men remarked of her, 'She should have been a man.'

[2] The difference in orientation described here is perhaps also characteristic of American class systems. W. L. Warner and P. S. Lunt, *op. cit.*, remark (page 89) that 'Women were very conscious of class in Yankee City'.
See also T. Parsons, 'An Analytical Approach to the Theory of Social Stratification', *Amer. Jour. Soc.*, Vol. XLV, 1940.

I married and said she would never marry a working man. But I had the last laugh for she got landed too and had to marry (a working man).'

I do not mean that the sexes exhibit exclusively different orientations, only that women value status more than men while men value esteem more than women. Most working men (to quote one) 'are content to be where they are; they want more money and higher wages, of course, but they've no desire to rise up. I'll tell you where the trouble starts, it's when a working lassie marries a man higher than herself; then she's not content but wants to go on. . . .'

Neither different orientation nor different positions with respect to status and esteem by themselves explain the greater success of women in upward mobility. To take the analysis further another structural feature of rural society has to be considered, that is relations between members of the same sex but of different social classes. Here I shall consider the two middle classes as one, since the majority of the men in them stand over against working men in their capacity of employers and property owners. Working class men and middle class men stand in a relationship of opposition – the point has been stressed in an earlier chapter. On the other hand there is nothing in the role of the women of the two classes to bring them into opposition and instead middle class women stand in a relation of patronage to working class women. Working class men through their unions are consciously united in opposition to middle class men, while the women are not. The men are forced to reject the middle class while women need not.

The different relationships are apparent in many features of social life but are seen most strikingly in the formal associations of the community (apart from church). Membership of these by class and sex is as follows:

Bowling Club (Men only)	All working class men (except one who rarely attends).
Badminton Club (Men and women)	Lower-middle class couples.
	Lower-middle class youths (both sexes).
	Working class wives (a few).
	Working class girls.
	One working class schoolboy.

Dramatic Club (men and women)	Lower-middle class males and females Working class women. One working class man.
Women's Rural Institute (women only)	All three classes equally represented.
Women's Church Guild (women only)	Working class and lower middle (occasionally a representative of upper middle).
The Brownies (women only)	All three represented.

It is apparent that in these associations in the parish where the middle class is represented few or no working class men are members, while the presence of middle class persons in an organization is no deterrent to working class women.

The patronage relation of the woman is also illustrated by these clubs. The leaders (as described earlier) are all of the middle classes and make no secret of the fact that they conceive the purpose of the clubs to be to 'do things for' the working class women, or their children in the case of the Brownies. I wish to make it clear that by 'patronage relation' I mean action of this sort, and not a 'patronizing attitude' – this latter is never overtly expressed. A middle class woman often enters into a non-reciprocal relation with some one working class woman, usually a husband's employee's wife. For example she will pass on old clothes to the working class woman and sometimes lend her one of her own dresses for a special occasion. Usually in such a relationship the middle class woman will occasionally drop in on the working class woman for tea and talk, without being invited and without asking or permitting a return visit.

The difference in relation between men of the two classes and women of the two classes is reflected in numerous culture traits. In style of adornment, manners and speech working class women resemble middle class women much more than working class men resemble middle class men. Without photographs and recordings it is difficult to demonstrate this, but the interview material given below shows that this is not a 'subjective impression' on my part but is also a judgment of middle class women. An interesting illustration in speech is that many middle class men have two dialects – the anglicized middle class one they use in the home and in talking to persons of equal status, and one resembling working class dialect for use in the fields and with their own men. In the steading a farmer will say to his men e.g. 'that corn'll no be wet?' and a minute later in his house will use the middle class construction 'it won't be' in speaking to his family. Middle class women however do not have two dialects; they do not need two, for though there is difference in accent between the women of the two classes (in some individuals there is not even this) there are few differences in vocabulary and construction. I have often heard working class mothers 'correcting' their children's speech, i.e. changing it from dialect to the sort used in school, but never working class fathers.

In talking of differences between the classes, middle class women (especially lower-middle class) stress the importance of manners. For the purpose in hand it is enough to accept their standpoint that manners are ways of treating others which they themselves use, but which working class women do not use so much and which working class men use hardly at all. To pick one's nose or to spit when in the presence of another is bad manners from a middle class point of view, and they never do it. Neither do working class women, but working class men do often. The same pattern holds for swearing, use of handkerchiefs, and, particularly important, the use of the terms of address and reference 'Mr' and 'Mrs'. These are important because as a result of the pattern described 'Mr' is a class symbol while 'Mrs' is not. Working class women use 'Mrs' among themselves when addressing or referring to appropriate persons (someone not intimately related to the speaker) in all classes, while, as described, working class men only use 'Mr' of middle class men. These cultural differences are reflected in a feeling working class men have that middle class men are slightly effeminate, since their manners are like those of the women of both classes.

That the distance between the sexes in the working class, their different orientation and the very different relationship with members of the same sex in the middle class result in the women being in a more favourable position for upward mobility, is shown in the following interview. I asked a middle class woman if she would attempt to control her daughter's choices when she reached courting age; she replied:

'I should be diplomatic, but I should be sorry to see her make a hash of her choice.'

J.L. 'What do you consider a hash?'

'If she formed an attachment with one of the cottagers, working lads, like X or Y; they're fine young men, but wouldn't make her happy. They haven't the background of culture and thought that she has . . . Probably for (my son) it's rather different; the (working class) girls here have greater refinement of manners and appearance than the boys. You've only to see them on the bus or changing at dances to see how nice and wholesome they are. So *that* I should consider.'

An upper middle class woman extolled the virtues of a maid she had had . . . 'she could go anywhere but she'd need to learn of course. I would like to take her to London and show her things, for she's so appreciative. I told my nephew he should book her (for a wife). She was so clever at learning things – it's curious how a girl will take polish when a man won't'. She went on to compare the girl with her brother, who was 'gauche and crude', to illustrate her last point.

These differences between male and female in the working class are found to some extent among children above the age of ten as well as in adults. Schoolchildren between ten and twelve were asked what occupation they wanted: half the girls wanted jobs which provided a definite status gain over parents' present one, while only one of the boys did. The most favoured occupation of the girls was school teaching; the boys wanted either agricultural work or 'working in a garage' with a single exception who wanted to be a fighter pilot.[1] The children were told a story of a shepherd who courted a farmer's daughter whose parents would not allow him to marry her and who was killed in a fight with her brother. No motivations were given in the story and the children were then questioned about the motives of the characters. To the question why the parents would not allow the marriage most of the girls answered 'because he was a shepherd' while most of the boys answered 'because the brother didn't like him.' Several parents commented on the fact that daughters became aware of class differences and barriers by about fourteen while their sons did not until four to five years later.

Children are treated by their elders in ways consistent with these differences. Boys are treated by the men in a jokingly

[1] Probably more because of the esteem to be won than of status to be gained.

aggressive way – the boys' achievements, performances and property are belittled in a blunt humourous manner, often leading to
mock fights which the boys of course lose. This continues up to
about fifteen when the boys start working. By this treatment they
are being told they have yet to make the grade as tough skilled
males. Girls are either ignored by the men or treated in a kindly
almost sentimental manner; from the age of about ten they are
given occasional charge of babies either in their own house or a
neighbour's, while their mothers start to induct them into house-
work. By fifteen they are expected to be able to run the normal
house routine and at the same time they begin to learn the more
social skills.

There are indications that the configuration of relationships
described above is changing. In the working class the distance
between the sexes is narrowing and the male is becoming less
dominant. For example young wives now often refuse to live in
'outbye' cottages (cottages situated far from the road – see next
chapter) and will not let their husbands take employment which
involves living in one of them; some will not permit their husbands to take employment which involves living in cottages without electric light and a hot water system. Amongst those above
forty, male and female tasks are sharply separated – the woman
for example does all the house work, rearing of children, feeding
of chickens and milking of cows. The man does the heavy garden
work, pig killing and curing as well as his paid job. Below that
age these tasks are not amongst all couples specifically allotted
to either sex, the general direction of the change being that the
male takes over tasks formerly left to the female. In this type of
social situation there is always the danger that the observer
attributes change when in fact there are only differences between
one age grouping and another. However in this case parishioners
themselves note that a change is occurring. An elderly lady says
'wives don't do as much as they used to – milking and helping
in the garden and that. They stand in the garden with their arms
folded and tell their husbands what to do. I can't thole them'.
One young man described an uncle's relationship with his wife
. . . 'he's one of the old type – you know – you do your work
and I'll do mine and that's that.' He added that there were 'still
plenty like him', and thought that it was ex-servicemen who
were the agents of this change.

The analysis of the configuration of relationship in this section is partly corroborated by a recent study of urban families by Dr E. Bott devoted largely to conjugal roles[1]. She found that the degree of segregation in the role relationship of husband and wife varies directly with the connectedness of the family's social network. The family's social network consists of kinsfolk and friends; where these are in constant contact with each other (and with the spouses) there is a high degree of role segregation between husband and wife. Even in urban areas where there is little trace of the community on which a family's network must necessarily be founded, Bott concluded that 'families with close-knit networks are likely to be working class',[2] i.e., working class families are likely to show a marked degree of role segregation. Dr Bott adds that not all (urban) working class families will have close-knit networks; in this connection she explicitly draws attention to the difference between rural and urban society, pointing out that in rural society the family cannot escape being embedded in a close-knit network. This is true to some extent, but as I have described above, applies more to the working class than to the others. Members of the working class have more relatives within the parish than the middle classes, live within a more contained close-knit network. Lest my intentions in this section be misunderstood, however, I wish to add that I have been analysing the relationship between sex and class in a rural community and not offering hypotheses concerning the roles of husband and wife.

There is one problem implicit in this chapter which I wish to mention though I cannot deal with it. The men of the two classes will not meet in voluntary associations within the parish, but seem willing to do so outside, in the British Legion and in the Masons. While the number who attend these from the parish is extremely small, less than a dozen in each case, nevertheless that they do may indicate a willingness to associate together in a context not defined as a local one. For both these branch associations draw their membership from several parishes and villages. That large numbers attend them and that some will be strangers to each other might mean that it is easier for participants to drop the roles of employer and employee and meet on

[1] E. Bott, *Family and Social Network*, London, 1957.
[2] E. Bott, *op. cit.*, page 112.

some basis less constricted by possibilities of antagonism. It could however also mean the opposite, the large numbers of persons in each of the two roles supplying a demonstration of its power in which the individual can find security. However I cannot within the scope of a community study either adequately formulate the question implicit in these remarks, far less find the data to answer them. That parishioners wish to free themselves from such status as locality confers is made clear in the following chapter.

CHAPTER VIII

THE PARISH AND THE TOWN

IN earlier chapters I described the history of the parish, characterized by a relative loss of administrative, economic and social
self-sufficiency and the induction of parishioners into a more
dispersed network of social relations. One aspect of this change
was that contact between parishioners and nearby towns had
increased. In this last chapter I shall examine the relationship
between the country parish and the town in the light of the
social structure of the parish.

Dominance of the town characterizes the relationship between it and the rural parish. This dominance is most dramati-
cally expressed in the phenomenon of 'rural depopulation', the
rejection of the countryside as a place to live in by people
previously resident there in favour of some town. The Registrar
General for Scotland notes in his report for 1951 – 'The population resident in rural areas in Scotland was 1,150, 252 in 1901
or 25.7 per cent of the population of Scotland at that time. In
1951 it had fallen, notwithstanding the increase in the Scottish
population in the meantime, to 869,157 or 17.1 per cent of the
total population of the Country.'[1] There are few county parishes
in which this population movement is not reflected. The figures
for Westrigg are as shown on the next page.

These figures do not measure a migration of persons from
rural to urban areas. They also reflect e.g. a decrease in fertility,
family size having declined in rural areas over the period considered as it has in the population as a whole.[2] However, it is
well known that migration from rural areas to urban has been
a feature of the national social life for over a century now and
its original causes are obviously bound up with the growth and

[1] Census of Scotland, 1951, H.M.S.O.
[2] Census of Scotland, 1951, H.M.S.O.

TABLE 12

Population of Westrigg 1841 – 1951

Census Year	Total Population
1841	646
1851	672
1861	590
1871	551
1881	543
1891	488
1901	441
1911	392
1921	384
1931	372
1951	362

development of industry. I do not think however that the dominance of the town can be explained entirely on an economic basis at the present day. The reasons for this view are explained below. In this chapter I am not attempting to deal with migration itself; I am analysing the relationship between county parish and town, and migration merely figures here as one expression of the dominance of the town.

The dominance of the town is expressed not only by a movement of population from the countryside to towns, but also in the distinction made between townsmen and countrymen and in the attitude of mingled pity and derision which the former adopt towards the latter. The stereotype of the countryman is summed up in the term 'yokel', the dictionary definition of which is: 'Yokel; 1812. (origin obsc.). A countryman, rustic; a country bumpkin.' The term is a somewhat derogatory one evoking an image of a dull-witted, inarticulate, slow-moving creature. This is the picture townspeople of Broadfield and Craigton have of the inhabitants of Westrigg – not that these townspeople know the parish and its inhabitants very well, for it is surprising how many in the towns have never been in Westrigg. This in itself is an indication of the relationship between the two towns and the parish, for there are few parishioners who do not visit the towns fairly regularly. However, the picture townspeople have of parishioners was aptly summed up by a Broadfield man[1] as follows: 'We (of Broadfield) think that they (of Westrigg) are all sort of daft – I don't mean mental – but just, well, they don't know how to behave properly.'

It seems that the townsman's attitude described seems to arise in any society which has reached a high stage of urbanization. Nadel writes of the Nupe of West Africa: '. . . . the commoner of the town, the people of no name and title, rank higher than the people outside the capital, with their petty village titles and affairs. The citizens of Bida look down upon "the heathen" in the village, ridiculing their habits and character, their fashions and the way they talk, their lack of education and "urbanity" .'[2]

Other evidence will be given below showing that this attitude towards countrymen is widespread among townsmen. For the moment I wish to stress that country people are aware of these judgments, and are forced to deal with them. That is, they are forced to deal with the knowledge that a majority thinks of them as somewhat inferior to themselves. They are perfectly sophisticated about it, as the following conversations show. It would in fact be strange if they were not sophisticated about it since articles in the press discussing the rival merits of life in the town and in the country are by no means uncommon. These discussions usually present the matter as an issue – 'Is it better to live in the country or the town?' on which a person must come to a decision. The Westrigg Women's Rural Institute held a debate on this very subject a few years ago, voted 50-50 on it, and all went home to bed.

Here are examples of country people talking about townsmen's attitude to them. A shepherd says of townsmen: 'People think we're mugs, yokels, we country workers, but we're not.' He told how a transport driver passing through that morning had told him he was a mug to stay in a place like Westrigg and work at shepherding, and the long argument they had had. A ploughman talks of the shopkeepers of Craigton: 'They're good to country folk, they'll give us things under the counter the Craigton folks can't get.' (He laughs ironically). 'They think we've

---

[1] There are of course differences between age groups in the prevalence of such attitudes in them. The utterence quoted was by a man between 25–30 years.

[2] S. F. Nadel, *A Black Byzantium*, O.U.P., 1942, page 131.

such a hard time of it up in Westrigg we deserve a good turn now and then.'[1] An ex-serviceman tells us how he arrived in London for the first time and was persuaded to buy articles and services he didn't want: 'They saw I was a mug straightaway. I was green, fresh from the country. Even in wee places like Broadfield and Gordon', he added, 'they know you're from the country – maybe it's the bronzed complexion or something (said ironically) and as soon as they see you they start talking about the crops or something.' A young couple early in my fieldwork asked me how I liked the country, the wife saying that I would find the country strange and probably dislike it. I said I'd found it interesting so far. The husband sat up in his chair with a pleased smile and said there was always something interesting to see in the country if you cared to look for it. 'The trouble with most townspeople is they aren't interested in us, so we aren't interested in them, so when they come here they never find out anything interesting and get bored.' He went on to say how much he resented 'people' being interested in 'the country' at the present moment only because food was short, whereas before the war 'the country was neglected.'

Their sophistication is also displayed in the following incident. An Indian pedler came round the parish selling linen articles. Shortly after, I was speaking to a young working class housewife, who asked had I brought anything from the pedlar? I said no, and she said she hadn't either. I said his prices were too high for me. She said his prices were too high for her too and added with energy and aggression, 'They're all the same these pedlars, they just think we country people don't know what the right prices are.' Shortly after this I learned from one of the housewife's relatives that she (the housewife) had bought over two pounds worth of goods from the pedlar. In other words, all the time she had been speaking to me she had simply been trying to destroy a conception of herself which she feared I (a townsman) might have of her – a conception of herself as one ignorant of the right price of linen goods, a country person.

The reason the townsman gives for his attitude is that the country people are 'mugs' or at least unfortunate because they have to live in the countryside, and the countryside (especially

[1] This was at a time when many goods were still in short supply, and some were rationed.

Westrigg) is 'isolated', 'wild', or 'uncivilized'. The tradesmen from the towns were constantly asking me how I could bear to live in the place. For example, 'I don't know how you can stick it up here. There's no life up here. You hardly see a soul' (a butcher). A tradesman in town said 'I don't know how they manage to live up there – but it's not a living, only an existence. They never see anybody from one day to another, except their neighbours.' Another, 'It's an uncivilized place. There's nothing to do, and hardly a soul in the place.' An elderly parishioner told how when town friends of hers visit her they say, 'What do you do up here? How can you bear it? You never see anybody hardly. There's no picture house, no nothing.' To be 'isolated' means not to be able to associate with other people in large numbers, in cinemas, pubs and streets. Without such association one cannot be 'alive'. This is the townsman's view.

I have already shown that countrymen are aware of the townsmen's attitude to them. Whether the distinction between the two can be called a status difference is open to question, but certainly the attitude of the townsman is that the countryman is inferior to himself, that his conditions of life are inferior to his own. Not only are countrymen aware of this attitude but they accept the low valuation of 'isolation' on which the townsman's attitude is based.

Before going on to show this more precision must be introduced into the analysis by relating the material presented above to the social structure of the parish. So far in this chapter I have talked of 'countrymen' or 'parishioners' as if they were an undifferentiated population. Migration from country to town is however confined almost solely to the working class. The Social Survey in its examination of depopulation in the Solway Counties remarks: 'Within agriculture, farmers, bailiffs and foreman showed the smallest proportion of potential migrants (four per cent) of all occupations.'[1] In Westrigg, the few examples of actual transfer of residence from the parish to the town which occurred while fieldwork was in progress, five in all, were all of working class people.

Rural depopulation is almost exclusively a working class phenomenon, not because there are so many more of them than

[1] Bertram Hutchinson, *Depopulation and Rural Life in Scotland*, H.M.S.O., 1950, page 15.

of any other class, for the opposite trend is apparent in the upper-middle class. In Westrigg and in every adjoining parish are two or three upper-middle class farmers who have recently taken up residence (and work) in the country rather than the town by an act of choice. In Westrigg, two ex-civil servants and a ship-owner have bought farms and settled on them; in 'X', lower down the valley, a stockbroker and an ex-chartered accountant; in 'Y', a member of a whisky distilling firm and an ex-navy commander. That this trend is not confined to Westrigg and district is confirmed by a local banker and an agent of a fodder supply company.

Similarly the disparaging attitude to countrymen and the countryside is characteristic only of the town working class. Middle class people in town, on the other hand, often expressed envy of the independence and open-air life of the farmer. The farmers in Westrigg do not feel called upon to defend them-selves against a charge of being mugs, presumably because such a charge is never made against them. Nor do they feel obliged to defend themselves against the judgment that they live in an isolated place, for they have less difficulty in getting away from it. While discussing labour shortage, one remarked that 'they' (the working people) 'complain that this is an isolated place. It isn't – it only takes me two hours in the car to get to Edinburgh.' Another in a similar context remarked that he couldn't under-stand why 'people' said Westrigg was an isolated place since when he was in top form he could reach Edinburgh in one hour fifty minutes. That working people cannot jump into a car any afternoon did not seem to occur to them. In short, the rejection of the countryside as an habitat is mainly a working class characteristic. One or two of the working men were somewhat resentful that rural depopulation should be regarded as a 'prob-lem' (i.e., as something that should be stopped) pointing out that 'It's all right to say the country's a great place if you own a farm, but it's not much fun if you don't.' 'If people don't want to live in the country, its nobody's business but their own.'

Working class countrymen accept the same values on which the derogatory attitude of the town working class to countrymen is based. This is seen in their evaluation of the location of dwell-ing houses in the parish.

This evaluation hinges on a distinction between habitations

from which association with other people is easy and those from which it is not. The meaning of the two terms used in verbalizing this distinction must be explained, 'in-bye' and 'out-bye'. The terms are used in the first place to distinguish two types of land; in-bye land being the fields and out-bye the hill grazing land. The terms are used in a relative sense according to the unit of land referred to. Thus the two types are distinguished on a single farm; similarly an arable farm on the plains of the county will be distinguished as a whole from a hillsheep farm in Westrigg as a whole, by being called an in-bye farm as opposed to the Westrigg out-bye farm; similarly the whole upland parish of Westrigg is contrasted with any lowland parish in the same terms.

The primary meaning is extended to things associated with the two types of land, principally stock and habitation. Several farmers pasture a small flock of sheep on their fields; these are called 'in-bye' sheep and are kept strictly separate from the hill sheep. When applied to dwellings the terms not only distinguish but also evaluate, and to call a cottage 'out-bye' is to pass a depreciatory judgment on it.

Here are some of the associations the terms have for the inhabitants of the upland parish. The one land consists of fields lying at the side of the road or visible from it. The fields are worked upon by men, are protected by hedges, dykes, woods; they are more productive than the hills. In-bye sheep are always bigger, heavier, more valuable animals than the hill sheep, which are often brought down from the hills and grazed in the fields for a day or two before being sent to market, in order to acquire a healthy bloom. In a snowstorm the field sheep rarely require protection, unlike the hill sheep. Casualties are expected among the hill sheep but not among the field sheep. The hills are bare and treeless and can be dangerous in winter; an out-bye cottage is sometimes cut off from the rest of the world for a few days by flood or snowstorm. Yet a cottage need not be situated in the hills for it to be condemned as out-bye. An out-bye dwelling is any one which, for whatever reason, is 'isolated', one from which it is difficult to contact other people.

Verbal judgments on outlying cottages are often made by roadside dwellers which indicate their attitude. For example, I remarked to a shepherd's wife one day that I was going to visit a cottage four miles away in the hills, and two miles from its nearest neighbour. She replied in a horrified tone that she wouldn't live there 'for anything'. Several natives of the parish have never been out to this particular cottage. Walking the hill one day with a shepherd we saw in the distance another out-bye cottage, 'how would you like to be stuck out here all your bloody life?' he asked grimly. On a car tour of the borders with an elderly shepherd once he pointed to a desolate glen and saying that there was a cottage at the head of it, added, 'you'd have to be born in it to be able to live in a place like that.'

One summer a family moved from a cottage near the road to one several miles from it. This move was a topic of conversation for several months; parishioners were amazed, teased some of the family about it and made comments such as:

A seventy-year-old woman: '. . . a bad move that. And they could have got a place nearer the road if they'd wanted.'

A young tractor driver: 'Aye, it's a bit far out. It isn't a great place to go to.'

A thirty-year old shepherd: 'A bad move that. You'd have thought they'd want to be nearer the road.' His wife made similar remarks.

A fifty-five year-old woman: 'Isn't it terrible? I wouldn't like to live there.'

Two of these comments came from relatives of the family concerned. All occurred in informal talk.

Out-bye dwellers are aware of the judgment passed on their dwellings by the others and feel obliged sometimes to defend themselves from it. People are identified (in this context) with their dwellings and accordingly a distinction is felt to exist between in-bye dwellers and out-bye dwellers. For example the housekeeper at a cottage three miles from the road telling me about 'the people down there' (by the roadside) said, 'You've got to watch your step down there, there's three or four of them run the place and if you get on the wrong side of them you're finished.'[1] An out-bye shepherd said 'when you go down into Westrigg' (his cottage is in the parish) 'you'd think you came from a foreign country the way people treat you, "how're you gettin' on up there?" they say, you just about need a passport.' When mimicking the people asking he screwed up his face and

[1] The imputation here is quite unfounded.

nodded his head and used a patronizing tone of voice. The dis-
tiction is expressed by in-bye dwellers in ways which make it
clear that they think of themselves as being in some sense superior to out-bye dwellers – the latter not only are deprived of the
right to associate and communicate with others, it is said, but
also in time they lose the ability for it. They become 'backward'
i.e., are unable to interact readily.

For example a herd discussing the matter said '. . . in the past
and even up to just before the war people lived in these out-bye
places 'cos they knew no better. They never saw anybody.
Before the war when you went to visit them or went near some
of the out-bye places you never saw the kids. They all hid when
they saw you coming. You saw them keekin' out behind the
curtains or somewhere. They grew up shy and backward.' A
doctor (new to the district) remarked that a family of out-bye
dwellers regarded him with suspicion and he suspected that they
did not follow his instructions; an in-bye dweller explained to
him that 'people who have lived in an out of the way place as
long as they have become queer; they get queer ideas, and they
don't know how to treat people.'

This low evaluation of isolation is not simply a matter of talk.
The following table listing all but two shepherd's cottages shows
the distance of each cottage from the road and the number of
times it has vacated between 1940 and 1950. While one or two
out-bye cottages have not been vacated at all during this period
it is clear that they are more often vacated than the others.[1]

These out-bye cottages are in as good condition as the in-bye
ones. This is stressed because several writers on rural depopulation assert that bad housing is a major cause of it.[2]

Two points must be made clear here. First that in-bye and
out-bye are relative terms, and not absolute discriminations.
Thus the majority of people living in cottages at the roadside in
Westrigg think of themselves as in-bye dwellers in relation to
parishioners living in cottages some distance from the main road.

[1] The Department of Agriculture for Scotland estimate that the average
length of service in the same job is just over six years for shepherds.

[2] B. Hutchinson, *op. cit.*, seems to incline to this view at one point in his
study. See also G. D. Mitchell, 'Depopulation and Rural Social Structure',
Soc. Rev., 1950. A good discussion of the phenomenon of rural depopulation
is to be found in J. Saville, *Rural Depopulation in England and Wales, 1851–1951*,
Routledge & Kegan Paul, 1957.

TABLE 13

Cottage	Distance from Road	No. of times vacated
A	4 miles	6
B	$3\frac{1}{2}$ miles	2
C	3 miles	0
D	$2\frac{1}{2}$–3 miles	3
E	$2\frac{1}{2}$–3 miles	1
F	$2\frac{1}{2}$ miles	4
G	2 miles	4
H	$1\frac{1}{2}$–2 miles	3
I	$1\frac{1}{2}$–2 miles	0
J	$1\frac{1}{2}$–2 miles	0
K	$1\frac{1}{2}$ miles	0
L	$1\frac{1}{2}$ miles	0
M	1–$1\frac{1}{2}$ miles	0
N	$\frac{1}{2}$ mile	2
O	$\frac{1}{2}$ mile	0
P	$\frac{1}{2}$ mile	1
Q	0	0
R	0	0
S	0	0
T	0	2
U	0	0
V	0	0

The people of Craigton on the other hand think of everyone in Westrigg as an out-bye dweller (though they do not always use that term). Thus whether a dwelling is thought of as isolated or not depends on the relation of the thinker to it. To a townsman of the working class all dwellings in Westrigg are isolated. To an inhabitant of Westrigg the roadside cottages are not isolated but the others are. Those who at any time dwell in the out-bye cottages either deny that they are out-bye or, as with two shepherds I knew, simply say that they prefer to live somewhat isolated from other people.

The second point is that this low evaluation of out-bye cottages is a fairly recent phenomenon in the country. Informants talking about the situation stress that up to about a generation ago out-bye cottages were more highly valued than the others and were often occupied by one shepherding family for generations, e.g., a female parishioner: 'In the old days the shepherds said they preferred the isolated cottages for then they didn't have any work around the steading. They were their own masters.' A farmer: 'At one time shepherds stayed a lifetime in out-bye places. But not now – just the change in people's way of living. They were happy there; they were their own boss.' The young herd quoted on backwardness: '. . . they grew up shy and backward, so the sons didn't know anything else and just followed in their father's footsteps.'

Townsmen of the working class regard Westrigg with horror as an isolated place, and the people in it as unfortunate for having to live there; countrymen themselves express a horror of isolation. Socially, isolation means not being able to associate with other people, and its causes may be various. So far I have considered only one cause of it, a geographical one. But it can be due to other causes, for example to long working hours. In this section other instances of country persons in a position of relative isolation will be examined, and again it will be apparent that these positions are being rejected.

Amongst rural occupations it seems that shepherding is being rejected. Table 8 (page 21) gave the age structure of the main rural occupations (for Scotland as a whole) showing that shepherding has proportionately fewer youths and more elderly men than the other agricultural occupations, though not fewer youths than forestry. The figures from Westrigg are too small to be of much significance, but seem to indicate that there shepherding is the least attractive to boys of all the rural occupations. The figures are as shown on opposite page.

These figures however, (both national and parish) have to be cautiously interpreted. Since it takes several years to learn shepherding and since it is a more responsible job (in the eyes of farmers) than the others, it is possible that boys learning the craft are either not entrusted with a hirstle or not granted the title of shepherd, or both, and hence are not included in official statistics. Or, above the age of 65 there are proportionately more shepherds than others, but this might be explained in the following way: shepherding cannot be done on a part-time basis but demands continuous knowledge and daily care of a flock, hence anyone employed in shepherding is on a full time basis and is bound to be included in official statistics; other agricul-

TABLE 14

Rural Occupations in Westrigg – Age Structure

Age	Shepherds	Agricultural Workers	Forestry Workers
15–19	0	4	4
20–24	4	3	0
25–29	4	1	3
30–34	1	2	8
35–39	6	2	5
40–44	2	1	2
45–49	4	2	1
50–54	3	2	3
55–59	0	1	0
60–64	4	3	2
65 +	5	2	1
totals	33	23	29

tural work has periods of intense activity (e.g., harvesting) when a lot of labour is required or at least is desirable, and periods of inactivity. In Westrigg (and no doubt elsewhere) retired agricultural workers over 65 are often hired on daily contract during the periods of intense activity, but since they draw the old age pension avoid being recorded as agricultural workers.

The evidence for a rejection of shepherding is perhaps rather to be found in an accumulation of local detail. For example, in Westrigg there are no boys under 20 learning the craft at present. On two farms are instances of one shepherd looking after a double hirstle, and having done so for some years. Of five shepherds' sons between 15 and 25 in the parish only one is himself a shepherd (very few men apart from shepherds' sons become shepherds, see page 118). Two of the shepherds above age 65 have wanted to retire but been persuaded by their farmers to stay on.

Finally, as evidence of this move away from shepherding there is the testimony of farmers and shepherds themselves and of official reports on the subject. Shepherds often remark that their craft seems to be dying out. Farmers too bemoan the difficulty of finding herds these days and in morose moments envisage the sheep farms having to be abandoned in a generation or two for lack of them. Finally, there are official reports from one of which only I shall quote, the Committee on the Development of the Scottish Borders, 'Labour shortage (in farming) is worst however on upland and hill farms, among stockmen, and especially shepherds.'[1]

Rural depopulation is a rejection of the status of working class countrymen. Any satisfactory explanation of it must also explain why the position of shepherd is more heavily rejected than any other within this category. An explanation of rural depopulation that is frequently put forward is that it is due to the low wages paid to the country worker in comparison with the town worker. This explanation is hardly convincing in view of the fact that the shepherd is the most highly paid of all the agricultural workers. The regular cash wage of agricultural workers varies a little from district to district, but the proportionate wage of any one class of worker relative to the others does not vary very much.

The official minimum wages over most of the Borders are:

| | AGE | | | | | |
	15–16	16–17	17–18	18–19	19–20	20 +
Male worker (general Worker)	46/3	54/–	62/3	75/–	91/9	108/–
Horsemen, tractormen, stockmen	50/3	61/–	70/3	83/6	100/3	117/6
Shepherds	51/3	62/3	71/3	85/6	102/6	120/–

What shepherds do complain of is that from the nature of their job they can rarely get away from the farm. The daily working hours of the other agricultural workers are specified for various periods of the year, but not for the shepherds. The relevant order on working hours merely remarks of shepherds:

Customary hours tending sheep and grazing stock.

In other words, no hours are laid down for the shepherd nor by the nature of his work could they be. It is about this that shep-

[1] The report is unpublished.

herds do complain, or rather when dicussing the advantages
and disadvantages of their job it is always this that is stressed
as the major drawback to it. For example, a young shepherd discussing rural depopulation said that many people preferred jobs
in towns because in them 'You have definite leisure hours, especially a free weekend you can count on having.' This was said
at ten o' clock at night while the two of us were gathering in
sheep from the hill preparatory to a sorting the following morning. 'Look at me', he added, 'I'm still at work at ten o' clock.' A
shepherd I met one Sunday evening doing his hill round similarly
mentioned the lack of specificity of working hours before wages
as a ground for dissatisfaction. 'The herd's tied to his work', he
said, 'even work on Sunday just now. That puts a lot off. I've a
brother in a steelworks used to be a shepherd. He says he's better
off now, gets his weekends free and bigger wages too, though he
doesn't make out any better than me.' Farmers give the same
reason for the shortage of herds. One of them remarked 'I don't
blame them, I don't think anyone wants to be tied at the week-
ends.'

In other words the shepherd is less able than other agricultural workers to get away from the farm and engage in activities
and associations of his own choice. He has less freedom to associate with whom he pleases. This is already implicit in some of
the quotations given, and is explicit in the following words of a
shepherd given in the course of an interview on how one learns
to be a shepherd. After describing how he helped his father at
lambing he went on to say that no boys he knew at school or
over school-leaving age were learning the craft now. Asked why
he replied that 'you can get into town more easily now . . . in my
young days a visit to town was an occasion. Of course it's worse
for shepherds than for ploughmen, for we work seven days a week
and they don't. Of course we have our slack time but we're
rarely *free* (his emphasis). What happens now is a shepherd goes
to town once in a while, meets pals who have leisure at week-
ends and the same wage or mebbe more, and he knows they have
leisure every weekend.'

There is a movement in Westrigg from one occupation to
another which confirms this interpretation, a movement of men
from shepherding and other agricultural work into forestry
labouring. Thus two G.A.W.'s were formerly shepherds, and

seven forestry labourers were formerly herds or ploughmen. There is no movement back from forestry into agriculture.

The significance of this movement for the theme of this chapter is that in it there is a progressive decrease in wages from shepherd to forestry labourers, but a progressive increase in calculable leisure time. The decrease in wages is shown on the table on page 150. Forestry labourers are paid at the same rate as 'general workers', the lowest agricultural rate.

There is another structural element in this situation which adds weight to the interpretation given, that is that wives are much more critical of the isolation of Westrigg than the husbands are, and that husbands often say that while they themselves are content to live in the parish 'it's harder on the wife, because she is tied to the house all day and never sees anybody.' while the husband associates with others in the course of his work. Indeed farmers say now that when they interview applicants for a job, it's the applicant's wife who really decides whether or not the man will take the new job, after having been given information about the location of the cottage the new job would entail. For example a farmer describes how he went to a town eighty miles away to interview a man he wanted to hire as a ploughman. 'It was all right while I spoke to him, and he seemed quite willing to take the job. Then his two daughters came in – he was a widower – and asked how far the cottage was from the nearest town, and what the bus services were like and so on and when I told them they flatly refused to come. So of course he couldn't either.' Another farmer: 'It was my ploughman's wife that persuaded him to leave me. She said the place was too out-bye.' Most farmers can tell of similar experiences. That it is harder on the wife is seen from the fact that a wife sometimes complains that her own cottage is 'out-bye' when the husband doesn't. Finally, the majority of shepherds in cottages in the hills are bachelors, the housekeeping being done by a widowed mother, a sister or a paid housekeeper. Farmers say it is difficult to get married shepherds to take jobs which entail living in these lonely dwellings.

One other recent event in the parish confirms this interpretation – the alacrity with which the girls employed as maidservants abandoned the job for work in the Broadfield mills as soon as the opportunity arose. For the maid-servant then was in the position of not having calculable leisure hours, whereas the mill girls' work stops every day at six o' clock. It is in fact this feature of the work which the girls stress when explaining why they changed so quickly. As one tersely put it, as a mill girl 'ye ken when ye're finished.'

The analysis so far shows that working class countrymen have accepted the town working class's low estimation of 'isolation', and that isolation means being restricted in one's association with others. Isolation has no absolute meaning but is contingent upon the possibilities of association with others. The contingencies limiting association are both physical and social – geographical location and occupation. However, the vast majority of countrymen are obviously more limited than townsmen.

The space of the isolation so far considered is a purely physical space – people are prevented by their position in physical space from meeting others. Social space is of a different nature and has to be described in terms of participation. It is difficult to separate the two types of space in analysis of rural-urban attitudes, but there is some evidence to suggest that in this situation limitations on social space are as important as those on physical.[1]

Despite the fact that everyday commercial ties between parishioners and Broadfield are more numerous than with Craigton, parishioners prefer to visit the latter. Now the difference between the two towns is simply that the latter is more 'townlike' than Broadfield. To say this is hardly illuminating but I shall try and isolate the difference between the two, which difference will indicate what I mean by 'townlike'.

It is sometimes said that country people migrate to towns because of the greater opportunities for entertainment in them. Yet there is no form of entertainment in Craigton which cannot be found in Broadfield. There is a cinema in both places, a dance hall in both, public houses and cafés in both. But there is this difference – that the area of choice is greater in Craigton, and this town has a more modern façade and copes with a greater number of people. Craigton is, in ecological terms, a 'centre of dominance' for a large area, whereas Broadfield to

[1] Cf. R. Firth, *Two Studies of Kinship in London*, London, 1956. Some of the effects of isolation of the individual on his health are discussed in W. Watson and M. Susser, *op. cit.*

quote a parishioner is a 'dead wee hole'. It has far fewer shops and pubs and cafés. Each town has one dance hall and one cinema. The Broadfield cinema building is a converted church hall, whereas the Craigton one was built as a cinema and except in size looks like any modern cinema. Similarly, several of the Craigton pubs have the glitter and shine of modern metropolitan pubs, but only one of the Broadfield ones has. The Craigton dance hall manages far more often to engage nationally celebrated country dance bands. In short, the difference between the two towns is not that one provides entertainment and the other does not, but that Craigton offers mingling with larger crowds of people, a greater range of choice, and an opportunity to participate in cultural forms, the styles of which are nearer to those found in large towns.

In short, by spending one's time in Craigton rather than in Broadfield one is affirming one's participation in a culture freer of local peculiarities of style than that of Broadfield, and one's capacity to enter into associations (however ephemeral) not determined by a narrow locality. A 'local community' it seems is not a group that anyone particularly wants to belong to.

My first chapters showed how the population of the local rural community was drawn into a wider, more extended network of relationships. This means that this population, brought into contact with a much wider range of persons than formerly, have been forced to compare their status and circumstances with that of others in the wider network, particularly townsfolk. It seems from the evidence presented that the parishioners have to a large extent accepted the evaluation of their status and circumstances which the others hold. This view I think is what a farmer was expressing when he said: 'In the old days you couldn't get anywhere, you just stayed here and you never knew anything else. So everyone was content. Now everywhere and everything's within reach, but because they (i.e., parishioners) know other people can get anything there's nobody contented now.'

The countrymen who actually do migrate to the town would in this view simply be those who have wholly accepted this evaluation. This seems consistent with the findings of the Social Survey that: 'It was fairly clear that potential migrants tended to regard their environment more critically than those who did

not wish to move', and 'what is strongly suggested by the anomalous and apparently inconsistent nature of some of the evidence
is that rural migration in many cases has sprung basically from
a general dissatisfaction with rural life rather than with one
or other aspect of it.'[1]

Studies of rural communities in Britain tend to emphasize
'these aspects of culture which distinguish (the community)
from large urban centres'[2] or to analyse mainly those interper-
sonal relationships based on bonds of kinship and neighbourhood which make up the local social network.[3] In this study the
emphasis has been rather on the similarity between Westrigg
and urban centres and on those relationships through which
parishioners participate in a more extended network of social
relations. It seemed to me to be necessary to treat the parish in
this way, partly because the farms there are enterprises in the
'agricultural industry' and not family farms, and partly because
the most significant social process in the recent history of the
parish has been its induction into the wider network.[4] Where
this process has advanced to the degree it has in Westrigg the
local community becomes less 'an area of common life', than an
area within which the individual chooses his associations subject
to such barriers as are imposed by social class or physical
distance. The people round him are no longer all actual neighbours but only possible neighbours. The locale itself ceases to be
the actual place where he lives and has his being and becomes
one possible place amongst others, to be compared and evaluated
with others.

[1] B. Hutchinson, *op. cit.*, pages 17 –18.
[2] W. M. Williams, *op. cit.*, page 200.
[3] As is so excellently done in R. Frankenberg, *op. cit.*
[4] The writers on rural sociology in Britain already mentioned, Arensberg,
Rees, Williams and Frankenberg, all note that this process is under way in
the communities they have studied.

APPENDIX I

ORGANIZATION OF THE SHEEP FARM

SHEEP in this district are kept for two purposes, the main one being for breeding lambs, the other for producing wool. The lambs are sold mainly to low-lying farms where they are fattened for the meat market or used to breed other strains of sheep. The main unit of organization on the hill sheep farm is the hirstle, an area of land with sheep on it under the charge of one shepherd; it may be up to about 1,200 acres in area with about 500 to 600 sheep on it. One sheep to just under two acres is the normal ratio. The largest farm in the parish has seven hirstles, the smallest has one.

The sheep on a hirstle between the end of the lamb sales and the beginning of the next lambing season are all breeding ewes (between October-May). Six years is held to be the most a ewe can stand in those exposed hills so every September the six year olds are sold and replaced by an equal number of lambs retained from that year's crop. The replacements, called 'hoggs' are not permitted to breed during their first year on the hirstle. In their second year they are called 'gimmers' and are specially watched and cared for at lambing time. A system of signs is used to indicate the place of each ewe in the six year cycle; every year the batch of hoggs is given a 'lug mark' – notches cut out the fore ear. Thus this year's hoggs may have no notches, next year's one, and so on up to four; no more than four are required since the difference between a six year old and a lamb is patent.

The flock on a hirstle is segmented into 'cutts'. These are smaller flocks each occupying a distinct territory, and varying in number from a few dozen animals to two hundred. A cutt moves round its territory seeking pasture as a unit; it is unusual for a sheep to stray into the company of another cutt, although it is one of the minor duties of the shepherd to see that they don't. If a flock is removed entirely from its hirstle – e.g. through disease – and a completely new stock has to replace it, the shepherd with assistants has to 'heft' the new stock in cutts to the hillsides. This requires that they stay constantly with the sheep for at least ten days and nights to prevent them straying from their allotted territories. The value of this organization is recognized commercially, if you buy a farm with stock already so organized you pay 10s a head of sheep over and above the agreed market value of the animals.

The functions of this organization are several but the main one is to control breeding. Farmers are against too close in-breeding of the animals, and while practice varies from farm to farm it can be taken that almost all farmers prevent the breeding of fathers with daughters and half-brothers with sisters. It is not practicable on these hill farms to bring the ewes into the fields during the breeding season (17 November – 31 December) for no farm has enough field acreage to contain them. Instead the tups are driven on to the hills. It is obvious that were the ewes not already organized in cutts it would be impossible to prevent random contact between tups and ewes, unless a new set of tups was used every second year. The latter possibility would be somewhat expensive, as a good tup costs anything from £30 – £1,000 and one tup can impregnate no more than 60–70 ewes in a season.

Each cutt is a breeding unit, a tup will not be used on two different cutts in one season. After being used for two seasons on one cutt the tup is moved to another one. In this way the tups are moved round the whole sheep population of the farm without the breeding rules being violated.

Parallels to this form of segmentation, intended to prevent random (sexual) contact which would negate mating rules, are perhaps to be found in some human societies. (See e.g., Radcliffe-Brown's 'Social Organization of Australian Tribes', *Oceania*, Vol. 1, 1931).

APPENDIX II

TECHNIQUES IN THE STUDY OF SOCIAL CLASS

THE techniques applied to the investigation of social class in the community were as follows. Having heard in the course of conversation with parishioners the three categories 'gentleman farmer', 'working farmer' and 'working folk' crop up with great frequency, and always with some tone of evaluation, I asked various informants for lists of persons who came under these categories. These lists agreed with each other to a remarkable extent, though it was noticeable that in this simple classification informants usually omitted to mention those persons whose class status later investigations showed to be somewhat ambiguous, such as some of the craftsmen.

From participation in and observation of the community at work and play I located as many of the friendships and cliques as I could. I checked the results with two parishioners who have lived in the community most of their lives and who have been in such positions as to have been able to observe the rest of the population. This took a great deal of time and was essential, yet the results are merely lists of names of no interest to the reader and are accordingly not presented here.

At meetings of such voluntary associations as I was permitted to join and at public entertainments I always noted who attended. As my knowledge of persons' associations was gradually added to in these ways it became clear that those persons not usually mentioned in local categorization, craftsmen and professional people, were distributed among the three categories. These were applied to public and private gatherings to determine their composition. Again a great deal of time was devoted to this and the result is a long list of such items as:

30 Dec.   Dance, about 200. All working folk except one forestry manager and one working farmer's daughter.

25 Aug.   Dance, about 50. All working folk.

24 Dec.   Christmas party, about 80. Working folk, 7 working farmers and family members, 4 forestry managers and family members, minister.

6 Jan.   Shooting party, 3. Gentlemen farmers.

30 July   Dinner party, 14. Gentlemen farmers.

Next, borrowing a device used by H. Kaufman (described in his *Prestige Classes in a New York Rural Community*, Agricultural Experiment Station, Cornell University Memoir 200) I wrote the name of each person, adults and children, separately on filing cards, and asked various informants to arrange the population into social classes, a separate pile of cards for each class. I gave no indication as to what I might mean by 'social class'. The results are shown in the table of class placements at the end of this appendix, with two exceptions. One is the placements of a working man who put the emphasis in the term on 'social' and arranged parishioners according to his estimate of their sociability and how much they contributed to the life of the community. The other is the placements of a woman in an equivocal position between lower middle and working class, who, in accordance with the emphasis on character and politeness already noted as a feature of the lower middle class arranged the population according to her estimate of them in those respects. These are omitted from the table not because I think they are less worthy of attention than the others but because they would complicate the presentation of the table unduly.

Finally, I held numerous interviews with informants on the subject.

(Double lines show ideas as

FIELDWORKERS SOCIAL CLASSES		INFORMANTS					
DESIGNATION	OCCUPATION	MR. A.	MRS. A.	MR. G.	REV. I.	MR. L..	MRS. N
THE A'S	FARMER	A	A	A	A	A	A
B'S	FARMER	B	B	B	B	B	B
C'S	FARMER	C	C	C	C	C	C
D'S	FARMER	D	D	D	D	D	D
E'S	FARMER	E	E	E	E	E	E
F'S	FARMER	F	F	F	F	F	F
G'S	FARMER	G	G	G	G	G	G
H'S	SCIENTIST	H	H	H	H	H	H
I'S	MINISTER	I	I	I	I	I	I
J'S	FARMER	J	J	J	J	J	J
K'S	RETIRED FARMER	K	K	K	K	K	K
L'S	FARMER	L	L	L	L	L	L
M'S	FARM MANAGER	M	M	M	M	M	M
N'S	SCHOOL TEACHER	N	N	N	N	N	N
O'S	SCHOOL TEACHER (retd.)	/	/	O	O	O	O
P'S	FORESTRY MANAGER	P	P	P	/	P	P
Q'S	FORESTRY MANAGER	Q	Q	Q	/	Q	Q
R'S	FARMER	R s t u	R	R	R	R	R
S'S	BLACKSMITH	⁰ X	⁰ X	X	ᵖᑫ X	S	S
T'S	TAILOR					X	T
U'S	JOINER						U + 3 other
X'S	REMAINING POPULATION						X

160

SOCIAL CLASSES

FOREST FOREMAN	SHEPHERD	SHEPHERD	CRAFTSMAN	CRAFTSMAN	COWMAN	SHEPHERD'S WIFE	COWMAN'S WIFE	FORESTER'S WIFE
A	A	A	A	A	A	A	A	A
B	B	B		B	B	B	B	B
C	C	C	C	C	C	C	C	C
D	D	D	D	D	D	D	D	D
E	E	E	E	E	E	E	E	E
F	F	F	F	F	F	F	F	F
G	G	G	G	G	G	G	G	G
H	H	H	H	H	H	H	/	H
I	I	I	I	I	I	I	/	I
J	J	J	/	J	J	J	J	J
K	K	K	K	K	K	K	HIK	K
L	L	L	L	L	L	L	L	L
M	M	M	M	M	M	M	M	M
N	N	N	N	N	N	N	N	R
O	O	O	O	O	O	O	O	NO
P	P	P	P	P	P	P	P	P
Q	Q	Q	Q	Q	Q	Q	Q	Q
R	R	R	R	R	R	R	R	/
S	S	X	/	/	X	S	S	X
X	T		T	T		T	X	
	U electrician		X	b X j		millgirls		
	X					forestry workers		

INDEX

The International Library of
Sociology
and Social Reconstruction

Edited by W. J. H. SPROTT
Founded by KARL MANNHEIM

ROUTLEDGE & KEGAN PAUL
BROADWAY HOUSE, CARTER LANE, LONDON, E.C.4

CONTENTS

PRINTED IN GREAT BRITAIN BY HEADLEY BROTHERS LTD
109 KINGSWAY LONDON WC2 AND ASHFORD KENT

GENERAL SOCIOLOGY

Brown Robert. Explanation in Social Science. *208 pp. 1963. 25s.*

Gibson, Quentin. The Logic of Social Enquiry. *240 pp. 1960. 24s.*

Goldschmidt, Professor Walter. Understanding Human Society. *272 pp. 1959. 21s.*

Homans, George C. Sentiments and Activities: Essays in Social Science. *336 pp. 1962. 32s.*

Johnson, Harry M. Sociology: a Systematic Introduction. *Foreword by Robert K. Merton. 710 pp. 1961. (2nd Impression 1962.) 42s.*

Mannheim, Karl. Essays on Sociology and Social Psychology. *Edited by Paul Keckskemeti. With Editorial Note by Adolph Lowe. 344 pp. 1953. 30s.*
Systematic Sociology: An Introduction to the Study of Society. *Edited by J. S. Erös and Professor W. A. C. Stewart. 220 pp. 1957. (2nd Impression 1959.) 24s.*

Martindale, Don. The Nature and Types of Sociological Theory. *292 pp. 1961. 35s.*

Maus, Heinz. A Short History of Sociology. *234 pp. 1962. 28s.*

Myrdal, Gunnar. Value in Social Theory: A Collection of Essays on Methodology. *Edited by Paul Streeten. 332 pp. 1958. (2nd Impression 1962.) 32s.*

Ogburn, William F., and **Nimkoff, Meyer F.** A Handbook of Sociology. *Preface by Karl Mannheim. 612 pp. 46 figures. 38 tables. 4th edition (revised) 1960. 35s.*

Parsons, Talcott and **Smelser, Neil J.** Economy and Society: A Study in the Integration of Economic and Social Theory. *362 pp. 1956. (2nd Impression 1957.) 35s.*

Rex, John. Key Problems of Sociological Theory. *220 pp. 1961. 25s.*

Stark, Werner. The Fundamental Forms of Social Thought. *280 pp. 1962. 32s.*

FOREIGN CLASSICS OF SOCIOLOGY

Durkheim, Emile. Suicide. A Study in Sociology. *Edited and with an Introduction by George Simpson. 404 pp. 1952. 30s.*
Socialism and Saint-Simon. *Edited with an Introduction by Alvin W. Gouldner. Translated by Charlotte Sattler from the edition originally edited with an Introduction by Marcel Mauss. 286 pp. 1959. 28s.*
Professional Ethics and Civic Morals. *Translated by Cornelia Brookfield. 288 pp. 1957. 30s.*

Gerth, H. H., and **Wright Mills, C.** From Max Weber: Essays in Sociology. *502 pp. 1948. (4th Impression 1961.) 32s.*

Tönnies, Ferdinand. Community and Association. *(Gemeinschaft und Gesellschaft.) Translated and Supplemented by Charles P. Loomis. Foreword by Pitirim A. Sorokin. 334 pp. 1955. 25s.*

SOCIAL STRUCTURE

Andrzejewski, Stanislaw. Military Organization and Society. *With a Foreword by Professor A. R. Radcliffe-Brown. 226 pp. 1 folder. 1954. 21s.*

Cole, G. D. H. Studies in Class Structure. *220 pp. 1955. (2nd Impression 1961.) 21s.*

Coontz, Sydney H. Population Theories and the Economic Interpretation. *202 pp. 1957. (2nd Impression 1961.) 25s.*

Coser, Lewis. The Functions of Social Conflict. *204 pp. 1956. 18s.*

Eisenstadt, S. N. From Generation to Generation: Age Groups and Social Structure. *374 pp. 1956. 42s.*

Kelsall, R. K. Higher Civil Servants in Britain: From 1870 to the Present Day. *268 pp. 31 tables. 1955. 25s.*

Ossowski, Stanislaw. Class Structure in the Social Consciousness. *212 pp. 1963. 25s.*

SOCIOLOGY AND POLITICS

Barbu, Zevedei. Democracy and Dictatorship: Their Psychology and Patterns of Life. *300 pp. 1956. 28s.*

Benney, Mark, Gray, A. P., and **Pear, R. H.** How People Vote: a Study of Electoral Behaviour in Greenwich, *Foreword by Professor W. A. Robson. 256 pp. 70 tables. 1956. 25s.*

Bramstedt, Dr. E. K. Dictatorship and Political Police: The Technique of Control by Fear. *286 pp. 1945. 20s.*

Crick, Bernard. The American Science of Politics: Its Origins and Conditions. *284 pp. 1959. 28s.*

Hertz, Frederick. Nationality in History and Politics: A Psychology and Sociology of National Sentiment and Nationalism. *440 pp. 1944. (4th Impression 1957.) 32s.*

Kornhauser, William. The Politics of Mass Society. *272 pp. 20 tables. 1960. 25s.*

Laidler, Harry W. Social-Economic Movements: An Historical and Comparative Survey of Socialism, Communism, Co-operation, Utopianism; and other Systems of Reform and Reconstruction. *864 pp. 16 plates. 1 figure. 1949. (3rd Impression 1960.) 50s.*

Mannheim, Karl. Freedom, Power and Democratic Planning. *Edited by Hans Gerth and Ernest K. Bramstedt. 424 pp. 1951. 35s.*

Mansur, Fatma. Process of Independence. *Foreword by A. H. Hanson. 208 pp. 1962. 25s.*

Myrdal, Gunnar. The Political Element in the Development of Economic Theory. *Translated from the German by Paul Streeten. 282 pp. 1953. (3rd Impression 1961.) 25s.*

Polanyi, Michael, F.R.S. The Logic of Liberty: Reflections and Rejoinders. *228 pp. 1951. 18s.*

Verney, Douglas V. The Analysis of Political Systems. *264 pp. 1959. (2nd Impression 1961.) 28s.*

Wootton, Graham. The Politics of Influence: British Ex-Servicemen, Cabinet Decisions and Cultural Changes, 1917 to 1957. *320 pp. 1963. 30s.*

FOREIGN AFFAIRS: THEIR SOCIAL, POLITICAL AND ECONOMIC FOUNDATIONS

Bonné, Alfred. The Economic Development of the Middle East: An Outline of Planned Reconstruction after the War. *192 pp. 58 tables. 1945. (3rd Impression 1953.) 16s.*

State and Economics in the Middle East: A Society in Transition. *482 pp. 2nd (revised) edition 1955. (2nd Impression 1960.) 40s.*

Studies in Economic Development: with special reference to Conditions in the Under-developed Areas of Western Asia and India. *322 pp. 84 tables. (2nd edition 1960.) 32s.*

Hughes, Everett C. French Canada in Transition. *252 pp. 49 tables. 16 figures. 4 maps. 1946. 16s.*

Mayer, J. P. Political Thought in France from the Revolution to the Fifth Republic. *164 pp. 3rd edition (revised) 1961. 16s.*

Schenk, H. G. The Aftermath of the Napoleonic Wars: The Concert of Europe—an Experiment. *250 pp. 17 plates. 1947. 18s.*

Schlesinger, Rudolf. Central European Democracy and its Background: Economic and Political Group Organization. *432 pp. 1953. 30s.*

Thomson, David, Meyer, E., and **Briggs, A.** Patterns of Peacemaking. *408 pp. 1945. 25s.*

Trouton, Ruth. Peasant Renaissance in Yugoslavia, 1900-1950: A Study of the Development of Yugoslav Peasant Society as affected by Education. *370 pp. 1 map. 1952. 28s.*

SOCIOLOGY OF LAW

Gurvitch, Dr. Georges. Sociology of Law. *With a Preface by Professor Roscoe Pound. 280 pp. 1947. (2nd Impression 1953.) 24s.*

Renner, Karl. The Institutions of Private Law and Their Social Functions. *Edited, with an Introduction and Notes by O. Kahn-Freund. Translated by Agnes Schwarzschild. 336 pp. 1949. 28s.*

CRIMINOLOGY

Cloward, Richard A., and **Ohlin, Lloyd E.** Delinquency and Opportunity: A Theory of Delinquent Gangs. *248 pp. 1961. 25s.*

Friedländer, Dr. Kate. The Psycho-Analytical Approach to Juvenile Delinquency: Theory, Case Studies, Treatment. *320 pp. 1947. (5th Impression 1961.) 25s.*

Glueck, Sheldon and **Eleanor.** Family Environment and Delinquency. *With the statistical assistance of Rose W. Kneznek. 340 pp. 1962. 35s.*

Grygier, Tadeusz. Oppression: a Study in Social and Criminal Psychology. *Foreword by Hermann Mannheim. 392 pp. 1954. 28s.*

Mannheim, Hermann. Group Problems in Crime and Punishment, and other Studies in Criminology and Criminal Law. *336 pp. 1955. 28s.*

Morris, Terence. The Criminal Area: A Study in Social Ecology. *Foreword by Hermann Mannheim. 232 pp. 25 tables. 4 maps. 1957. 25s.*

Spencer, John C. Crime and the Services. *Foreword by Hermann Mannheim. 336 pp. 1954. 28s.*

Trasler, Gordon. The Explanation of Criminality. *144 pp. 1962. 20s.*

SOCIAL PSYCHOLOGY

Barbu, Zevedei. Problems of Historical Psychology. *248 pp. 1960. 25s.*

Blackburn, Julian. Psychology and the Social Pattern. *184 pp. 1945. (6th Impression 1961.) 16s.*

Fleming, C. M. Adolescence: Its Social Psychology: With an Introduction to recent findings from the fields of Anthropology, Physiology, Medicine, Psychometrics and Sociometry. *271 pp. 2nd edition (revised) 1963. 25s.*
The Social Psychology of Education: An Introduction and Guide to Its Study. *136 pp. 2nd edition (revised) 1959. 11s.*

Fleming, C. M. (Ed.). Studies in the Social Psychology of Adolescence. *Contributions by J. E. Richardson, J. F. Forrester, J. K. Shukla and P. J. Higginbotham. Foreword by the editor. 292 pp. 29 figures. 13 tables. 5 folder tables. 1951. 23s.*

Halmos, Paul. Solitude and Privacy: a Study of Social Isolation, its Causes and Therapy. *With a Foreword by Professor T. H. Marshall. 216 pp. 1952. 21s.*
Towards a Measure of Man: The Frontiers of Normal Adjustment. *276 pp. 1957. 28s.*

Hollitscher, Walter. Sigmund Freud: An Introduction. A Presentation of his Theory, and a Discussion of the Relationship between Psycho-Analysis and Sociology. *140 pp. 1947. (2nd Impression 1950.) 12s.*

Homans, George C. The Human Group. *Foreword by Bernard DeVoto. Introduction by Robert K. Merton. 526 pp. 1951. (4th Impression 1963.) 35s.*
Social Behaviour: its Elementary Forms. *416 pp. 1961. 30s.*

Klein, Josephine. The Study of Groups. *226 pp. 31 figures. 5 tables. 1956. (3rd Impression 1962.) 21s.*

Linton, Ralph. The Cultural Background of Personality. *132 pp. 1947. (4th Impression 1958.) 16s.*
See also Yang, M.

Mayo, Elton. The Social Problems of an Industrial Civilization. With an appendix on the Political Problem. *180 pp. 1949. (4th Impression 1961.) 18s.*

Ridder, J. C. de. The Personality of the Urban African in South Africa. A Thematic Apperception Test Study. *196 pp. 12 plates. 1961. 25s.*

6

Rose, Arnold M. (Ed.). Mental Health and Mental Disorder: A Sociological Approach. *Chapters by 46 contributors. 654 pp. 1956. 45s.*
Human Behavior and Social Processes: an Interactionist Approach. *Contributions by Arnold M. Ross, Ralph H. Turner, Anselm Strauss, Everett C. Hughes, E. Franklin Frazier, Howard S. Becker, et al. 696 pp. 1962. 56s.*

Smelser, Neil J. Theory of Collective Behavior. *448 pp. 1962. 45s.*

Spinley, Dr. B. M. The Deprived and the Privileged: Personality Development in English Society. *232 pp. 1953. 20s.*

Wolfenstein, Martha. Disaster: A Psychological Essay. *264 pp. 1957. 23s.*

Young, Professor Kimball. Personality and Problems of Adjustment. *742 pp. 12 figures. 9 tables. 2nd edition (revised) 1952. (2nd Impression 1959.) 40s.*
Handbook of Social Psychology. *658 pp. 16 figures. 10 tables. 2nd edition (revised) 1957. (3rd Impression 1963.) 35s.*

SOCIOLOGY OF THE FAMILY

Banks, J. A. Prosperity and Parenthood: A Study of Family Planning among the Victorian Middle Classes. *262 pp. 1954. 24s.*

Chapman, Dennis. The Home and Social Status. *336 pp. 8 plates. 3 figures. 117 tables. 1955. 35s.*

Klein, Viola. The Feminine Character: History of an Ideology. *With a Foreword by Karl Mannheim. 256 pp. 1946. 16s.*

Myrdal, Alva and **Klein, Viola.** Women's Two Roles: Home and Work. *238 pp. 27 tables. 1956. (2nd Impression 1962.) 25s.*

Parsons, Talcott and **Bales, Robert F.** Family: Socialization and Interaction Process. *In collaboration with James Olds, Morris Zelditch and Philip E. Slater. 456 pp. 50 figures and tables. 1956. 35s.*

THE SOCIAL SERVICES

Ashdown, Margaret and **Brown, S. Clement.** Social Service and Mental Health: An Essay on Psychiatric Social Workers. *280 pp. 1953. 21s.*

Hall, M. Penelope. The Social Services of Modern England. *416 pp. 5th edition (revised) 1960. (2nd Impression 1962.) 28s.*

Heywood, Jean S. Children in Care: the Development of the Service for the Deprived Child. *256 pp. 1959. 25s.*

Jones, Kathleen. Lunacy, Law and Conscience, 1744-1845: the Social History of the Care of the Insane. *268 pp. 1955. 25s.*
Mental Health and Social Policy, 1845-1959. *264 pp. 1960. 28s.*

Jones, Kathleen and **Sidebotham, Roy.** Mental Hospitals at Work. *220 pp. 1962. 30s.*

Kastell, Jean. Casework in Child Care. *Foreword by M. Brooke Willis. 320 pp. 1962. 35s.*

Rooff, Madeline. Voluntary Societies and Social Policy. *350 pp. 15 tables. 1957. 35s.*

Shenfield, B. E. Social Policies for Old Age: A Review of Social Provision for Old Age in Great Britain. *260 pp. 39 tables. 1957. 25s.*

Trasler, Gordon. In Place of Parents: A Study in Foster Care. *272 pp. 1960. 25s.*

Young, A. F., and **Ashton, E. T.** British Social Work in the Nineteenth Century. *288 pp. 1956. (2nd Impression 1963.) 25s.*

SOCIOLOGY OF EDUCATION

Banks, Olive. Parity and Prestige in English Secondary Education: a Study in Educational Sociology. *272 pp. 1955. 25s.*

Collier, K. G. The Social Purposes of Education: Personal and Social Values in Education. *268 pp. 1959. (2nd Impression 1962.) 21s.*

Cumming, Ian. Helvetius: His Life and Place in the History of Educational Thought. *With an Introduction by Nicholas Hans. 288 pp. Frontispiece. 1 folder. 1955. 25s.*

Dale, R. R. From School to University: A Study with special reference to University Entrance. *288 pp. 23 tables. 1954. 21s.*

Edmonds, E. L. The School Inspector. *Foreword by Sir William Alexander. 214 pp. 1962. 28s.*

Evans, K. M. Sociometry and Education. *158 pp. 1962. 18s.*

Hans, Nicholas. New Trends in Education in the Eighteenth Century. *278 pp. 19 tables. 1951. 25s.*
Comparative Education: A Study of Educational Factors and Traditions. *360 pp. 3rd (revised) edition 1958. (2nd Impression 1961.) 23s.*

Jacks, M. L. Total Education: A Plea for Synthesis. *184 pp. 1946. (4th Impression 1955.) 16s.*

Mannheim, Karl and **Stewart, W. A. C.** An Introduction to the Sociology of Education. *208 pp. 1962. 21s.*

Ottaway, A. K. C. Education and Society: An Introduction to the Sociology of Education. *With an Introduction by W. O. Lester Smith. 212 pp. Second edition (revised). 1962. 18s.*

Peers, Robert. Adult Education: A Comparative Study. *398 pp. 2nd edition 1959. 35s.*

Pritchard, D. G. Education and the Handicapped: 1760 to 1960. *258 pp. 1963. 28s.*

Samuel, R. H., and **Thomas, R. Hinton.** Education and Society in Modern Germany. *212 pp. 1949. 16s.*

Simon, Brian and **Joan** (Eds.). Educational Psychology in the U.S.S.R. *Introduction by Brian and Joan Simon. Translation by Joan Simon. Papers by D. N. Bogoiavlenski and N. A. Menchinskaia, D. B. Elkonin, E. A. Fleshner, Z. I. Kalmykova, G. S. Kostiuk, V. A. Krutetski, A. N. Leontiev, A. R. Luria, E. A. Milerian, R. G. Natadze, B. M. Teplov, L. S. Vygotski, L. V. Zankov. 296 pp. 1963. 40s.*

Wittlin, Alma S. The Museum: Its History and its Tasks in Education. *328 pp. 24 plates. 18 figures. 1949. 28s.*

SOCIOLOGY OF CULTURE

Fromm, Erich. The Fear of Freedom. *286 pp. 1942. (8th Impression 1960.) 21s.* The Sane Society. *400 pp. 1956. (2nd Impression 1959.) 28s.*

Mannheim, Karl. Diagnosis of Our Time: Wartime Essays of a Sociologist. *208 pp. 1943. (7th Impression 1962.) 21s.* Essays on the Sociology of Culture. *Edited by Ernst Mannheim in cooperation with Paul Kecskemeti. Editorial Note by Adolph Lowe. 280 pp. 1956. (2nd Impression 1962.) 28s.*

Weber, Alfred. Farewell to European History: or The Conquest of Nihilism. *Translated from the German by R. F. C. Hull. 224 pp. 1947. 18s.*

SOCIOLOGY OF RELIGION

Argyle, Michael. Religious Behaviour. *224 pp. 8 figures. 41 tables. 1958. 25s.*

Knight, Frank H., and **Merriam, Thornton W.** The Economic Order and Religion. *242 pp. 1947. 18s.*

Watt, W. Montgomery. Islam and the Integration of Society. *320 pp. 1961. (2nd Impression.) 32s.*

SOCIOLOGY OF ART AND LITERATURE

Beljame, Alexandre. Men of Letters and the English Public in the Eighteenth Century: 1660-1744, Dryden, Addison, Pope. *Edited with an Introduction and Notes by Bonamy Dobree. Translated by E. O. Lorimer. 532 pp. 1948. 32s.*

Bruford, W. H. Chekhov and His Russia: a Sociological Study. *256 pp. 1948. 18s.*

Misch, Georg. A History of Autobiography in Antiquity. *Translated by E. W. Dickes. 2 Volumes. Vol. 1, 364 pp., Vol. 2, 372 pp. 1950. 45s. the set.*

Silbermann, Alphons. The Sociology of Music. *224 pp. 1963. 28s.*

SOCIOLOGY OF KNOWLEDGE

Hodges, H. A. The Philosophy of Wilhelm Dilthey. *410 pp. 1952. 30s.*

Mannheim, Karl. Essays on the Sociology of Knowledge. *Edited by Paul Kecskemeti. Editorial note by Adolph Lowe. 352 pp. 1952. (2nd Impression 1959.) 35s.*

Schlesinger, Rudolf. Marx: His Time and Ours. *464 pp. 1950. (2nd Impression 1951.) 32s.*

Stark, W. The History of Economics in its Relation to Social Development. *104 pp. 1944. (4th Impression 1957.) 12s.*
America: Ideal and Reality. The United States of 1776 in Contemporary Philosophy. *136 pp. 1947. 12s.*
The Sociology of Knowledge: An Essay in Aid of a Deeper Understanding of the History of Ideas. *384 pp. 1958. (2nd Impression 1960.) 36s.*
Montesquieu: Pioneer of the Sociology of Knowledge. *244 pp. 1960. 25s.*

URBAN SOCIOLOGY

Anderson, Nels. The Urban Community: A World Perspective. *532 pp. 1960. 35s.*

Ashworth, William. The Genesis of Modern British Town Planning: A Study in Economic and Social History of the Nineteenth and Twentieth Centuries. *288 pp. 1954. 25s.*

Cullingworth, J. B. Housing Needs and Planning Policy: A Restatement of the Problems of Housing Need and "Overspill" in England and Wales. *232 pp. 44 tables. 8 maps. 1960. 28s.*

Dickinson, Robert E. City Region and Regionalism: A Geographical Contribution to Human Ecology. *360 pp. 75 figures. 1947. (4th Impression 1960.) 25s.*
The West European City: A Geographical Interpretation. *600 pp. 129 maps. 29 plates. 2nd edition 1962. (2nd Impression 1963.) 55s.*

Dore, R. P. City Life in Japan: A Study of a Tokyo Ward. *498 pp. 8 plates. 4 figures. 24 tables. 1958. 45s.*

Gutkind, E. A. Revolution of Environment. *Demy 8vo. 476 pp. 32 plates. 60 figures. 3 folder maps. 1946. 32s.*

Jennings, Hilda. Societies in the Making: a Study of Development and Redevelopment within a County Borough. *Foreword by D. A. Clark. 286 pp. 1962. 32s.*

Kerr, Madeline. The People of Ship Street. *240 pp. 1958. 23s.*

Orlans, Harold. Stevenage: A Sociological Study of a New Town. *344 pp. 1 figure. 3 maps. 1952. 30s.*

RURAL SOCIOLOGY
(*Demy 8vo.*)

Bracey, H. E. English Rural Life: Village Activities, Organizations and Institutions. *302 pp. 1959. 30s.*

Infield, Henrik F. Co-operative Living in Palestine. *With a Foreword by General Sir Arthur Wauchope, G.C.B. 170 pp. 8 plates. 7 tables. 1946. 12s. 6d.*

Littlejohn, James. Westrigg: the Sociology of a Cheviot Parish. *5 figures. 1963. In Preparation.*

Saville, John. Rural Depopulation in England and Wales, 1851-1951. *Foreword by Leonard Elmhirst. 286 pp. 6 figures. 39 tables. 1 map. 1957. 28s. (Dartington Hall Studies in Rural Sociology.)*

Williams, W. M. The Country Craftsman: A Study of Some Rural Crafts and the Rural Industries Organization in England. *248 pp. 9 figures. 1958. 25s. (Dartington Hall Studies in Rural Sociology.)*
The Sociology of an English Village: Gosforth. *272 pp. 12 figures. 13 tables. 1956. (2nd Impression 1956.) 25s.*

SOCIOLOGY OF MIGRATION
(Demy 8vo.)

Eisenstadt, S. N. The Absorption of Immigrants: a Comparative Study based mainly on the Jewish Community in Palestine and the State of Israel. *288 pp. 1954. 28s.*

Little, Dr. K. L. Negroes in Britain: A Study of Racial Relations in English Society. *320 pp. 1947. 25s.*

Richmond, Anthony H. Colour Prejudice in Britain: A Study of West Indian Workers in Liverpool, 1941-1951. *212 pp. 3 figures. 25 tables. 1954. 18s.*

SOCIOLOGY OF INDUSTRY AND DISTRIBUTION
(Demy 8vo.)

Anderson, Nels. Work and Leisure. *280 pp. 1961. 28s.*

Blau, Peter M., and **Scott, W. Richard.** Formal Organizations: a Comparative approach. *Introduction and Additional Biography by J. H. Smith. 328 pp. 1963. 28s.*

Gouldner, Alvin W. Patterns of Industrial Bureaucracy. *298 pp. 1955. 25s.*
Wildcat Strike: A Study of an Unofficial Strike. *202 pp. 10 figures. 1955. 16s.*

Jefferys, Margot, with the assistance of Winifred Moss. Mobility in the Labour Market: Employment Changes in Battersea and Dagenham. *Preface by Barbara Wootton. 186 pp. 51 tables. 1954. 15s.*

Levy, A. B. Private Corporations and Their Control. *Two Volumes. Vol. 1, 464 pp., Vol. 2, 432 pp. 1950. 80s. the set.*

Levy, Hermann. The Shops of Britain: A Study of Retail Distribution. *268 pp. 1948. (2nd Impression 1949.) 21s.*

Liepmann, Kate. The Journey to Work: Its Significance for Industrial and Community Life. *With a Foreword by A. M. Carr-Saunders. 230 pp. 40 tables. 3 folders. 1944. (2nd Impression 1945.) 18s.*
Apprenticeship: An Enquiry into its Adequacy under Modern Conditions. *Foreword by H. D. Dickinson. 232 pp. 6 tables. 1960. (2nd Impression.) 23s.*

Smelser, Neil J. Social Change in the Industrial Revolution: An Application of Theory to the Lancashire Cotton Industry, 1770-1840. *468 pp. 12 figures. 14 tables. 1959. (2nd Impression 1960.) 40s.*

Williams, Gertrude. Recruitment to Skilled Trades. *240 pp. 1957. 23s.*

ANTHROPOLOGY
(*Demy 8vo.*)

Crook, David and **Isabel.** Revolution in a Chinese Village: Ten Mile Inn. *230 pp. 8 plates. 1 map. 1959. 21s.*

Dube, S. C. Indian Village, *Foreword by Morris Edward Opler. 276 pp. 4 plates. 1955. (4th Impression 1961.) 25s.*
India's Changing Villages: Human Factors in Community Development. *260 pp. 8 plates. 1 map. 1958. (2nd Impression 1960.) 25s.*

Fei, Hsiao-Tung. Peasant Life in China: a Field Study of Country Life in the Yangtze Valley. *Foreword by Bronislaw Malinowski. 320 pp. 14 plates. 1939. (5th Impression 1962.) 30s.*

Fei, Hsiao-Tung and **Chang, Chih-I.** Earthbound China: A Study of Rural Economy in Yunnan. *Revised English edition prepared in collaboration with Paul Cooper and Margaret Park Redfield. 346 pp. 7 plates. 50 tables. 1948. 20s.*

Gulliver, P. H. The Family Herds. A Study of Two Pastoral Tribes in East Africa, The Jie and Turkana. *304 pp. 4 plates. 19 figures. 1955. 25s.*
Social Control in an African Society: a Study of the Arusha: Agricultural Masai of Northern Tanganyika. *320 pp. 8 plates. 10 figures. 1963. 35s.*

Hogbin, Ian. Transformation Scene. The Changing Culture of a New Guinea Village. *340 pp. 22 plates. 2 maps. 1951. 30s.*

Hsu, Francis L. K. Under the Ancestors' Shadow: Chinese Culture and Personality. *346 pp. 26 figures. 1949. 21s.*
Religion, Science and Human Crises: A Study of China in Transition and its Implications for the West. *168 pp. 7 figures. 4 tables. 1952. 16s.*

Lin Yueh-Hwa. The Golden Wing: A Sociological Study of Chinese Familism. *Introduced by Raymond Firth. 264 pp. 1947. 18s.*

Lowie, Professor Robert H. Social Organization. *494 pp. 1950. (3rd Impression 1962.) 35s.*

Maunier, René. The Sociology of Colonies: An Introduction to the Study of Race Contact. *Edited and translated by E. O. Lorimer. 2 Volumes. Vol. 1, 430 pp., Vol. 2, 356 pp. 1949. 70s. the set.*

Mayer, Adrian C. Caste and Kinship in Central India: A Village and its Region. *328 pp. 16 plates. 15 figures. 16 tables. 1960. 35s.*
Peasants in the Pacific: A Study of Fiji Indian Rural Society. *232 pp. 16 plates. 10 figures. 14 tables. 1961. 35s.*

Osborne, Harold. Indians of the Andes: Aymaras and Quechuas. *292 pp. 8 plates. 2 maps. 1952. 25s.*

Smith, Raymond T. The Negro Family in British Guiana: Family Structure and Social Status in the Villages. *With a Foreword by Meyer Fortes. 314 pp. 8 plates. 1 figure. 4 maps. 1956. 28s.*

Yang, Martin C. A Chinese Village: Taitou, Shantung Province. *Foreword by Ralph Linton. Introduction by M. L. Wilson. 308 pp. 1947. 23s.*

DOCUMENTARY
(*Demy 8vo.*)

Belov, Fedor. The History of a Soviet Collective Farm. *250 pp. 1956. 21s.*

Meek, Dorothea L. (Ed.). Soviet Youth: Some Achievements and Problems. *Excerpts from the Soviet Press, translated by the editor. 280 pp. 1957. 28s.*

Schlesinger, Rudolf (Ed.). Changing Attitudes in Soviet Russia.
1. The Family in the U.S.S.R. *Documents and Readings, with an Introduction by the editor. 434 pp. 1949. 30s.*
2. The Nationalities Problem and Soviet Administration. Selected Readings on the Development of Soviet Nationalities Policies. *Introduced by the editor. Translated by W. W. Gottlieb. 324 pp. 1956. 30s.*

Reports
of the Institute
of Community Studies

(*Demy 8vo.*)

Jackson, Brian and **Marsden, Dennis.** Education and the Working Class: Some General Themes raised by a Study of 88 Working-class Children in a Northern Industrial City. *268 pp. 2 folders. 1962. (2nd Impression.) 28s.*

Marris, Peter. Widows and their Families. *Foreword by Dr. John Bowlby. 184 pp. 18 tables. Statistical Summary. 1958. 18s.*
Family and Social Change in an African City. A Study of Rehousing in Lagos. *196 pp. 1 map. 4 plates. 53 tables. 1961. 25s.*

Mills, Enid. Living with Mental Illness: a Study in East London. *Foreword by Morris Carstairs. 196 pp. 1962. 28s.*

Townsend, Peter. The Family Life of Old People: An Inquiry in East London. *Foreword by J. H. Sheldon. 300 pp. 3 figures. 63 tables. 1957. (2nd Impression 1961.) 30s.*

Willmott, Peter. The Evolution of a Community: a study of Dagenham after forty years. *168 pp. 2 maps. 1963. 21s.*

Willmott, Peter and **Young, Michael.** Family and Class in a London Suburb. *202 pp. 47 tables. 1960. (2nd Impression 1961.) 21s.*

The British Journal of Sociology. *Edited by D. G. MacRae. Vol. 1, No. 1, March 1950 and Quarterly. Roy. 8vo., £2 p.a.; 12s. 6d. a number, post free. (Vols. 1-11, £3 each.)*

All prices are net and subject to alteration without notice